WOMAN UP!

WOMAN UP!

YOUR GUIDE TO SUCCESS
IN ENGINEERING AND TECH

ANAT RAPOPORT

COPYRIGHT © 2023 ANAT RAPOPORT
All rights reserved.

WOMAN UP!
Your Guide to Success in Engineering and Tech

FIRST EDITION

ISBN   978-1-5445-4300-0 *Hardcover*
         978-1-5445-4299-7 *Paperback*
         978-1-5445-4301-7 *Ebook*
         978-1-5445-4302-4 *Audiobook*

To my family, whom I love most in this world.

To all those who trusted me with their stories as women in high tech.

Contents

INTRODUCTION 9

PART I: COMMON PROBLEMS
1. OBSTACLES FOR WOMEN 19
2. SELF-CONFIDENCE 31
3. IMPOSTER SYNDROME 37
4. NEGOTIATING SALARY 43
5. BUILDING A SUPPORT NETWORK 51
6. TOXIC ENVIRONMENTS 61
7. LEAVING THE WORKPLACE 69
8. MOTHERHOOD 79

PART II: SOFTWARE ENGINEERS
9. LOOKING FOR A JOB 91
10. TRANSITIONING SUCCESSFULLY TO YOUR NEW ROLE 103
11. RELATIONSHIPS WITH PEERS 109
12. RELATIONSHIPS WITH MANAGERS 117
13. HOW TO STAND OUT 129
14. CLIMBING THE LADDER WITHIN SOFTWARE ENGINEERING ... 137
15. HOW TO GET PROMOTED TO TEAM LEAD 157

PART III: TEAM LEADS

16. INTERVIEWING FOR AN EXTERNAL TEAM LEAD POSITION 167
17. ROLES AND RESPONSIBILITIES 175
18. TRAINING NEW EMPLOYEES 189
19. GROW TO YOUR NEXT POSITION 195

PART IV: MANAGERS

20. BUILDING YOUR MANAGER PERSONA 205
21. RECRUITING AND RETAINING EMPLOYEES 221
22. MANAGING OTHER MANAGERS 231

PART V: VPS OF R&D

23. ENTERING THE VP POSITION 239
24. WORKING WITH IMPORTANT STAKEHOLDERS 251
25. WORKING IN A STARTUP 259
26. SOME TECHNICAL ASPECTS OF YOUR JOB 269
27. MANAGING DATA SCIENCE 277
28. BEING A MEMBER OF COMPANY MANAGEMENT 285

CONCLUSION 291
ACKNOWLEDGMENTS 295
ABOUT THE AUTHOR 297

Introduction

In 2015, I was one of three engineering managers up for a promotion to director. Over the previous two years, I had worked hard to show myself capable. I had made personal changes that turned me into a better manager. My people were happy. My projects were succeeding. I was meeting deadlines.

Still, I felt like the VP held the power to dictate the next step in my career: if he *allowed* me to move up, great, otherwise it seemed like I would be stuck in a dead-end job without options.

I told a friend about the promotion and my concerns, and in response she said, "You have what it takes to be a senior manager, if not in this place, then somewhere else."

It was like a light bulb suddenly went on. My friend was absolutely right. If I didn't get the promotion here, I would find another way to move up to a director position. In fact, I didn't need to wait for this VP to think highly of me and make a decision. I could look outside my company *now* if I wanted to.

As I considered my friend's words over the following weeks, I realized that my career was not in the VP's hands. It was in mine. I wanted that promotion, and I was going to get it, whether at this company or somewhere else. *I* held the power to choose my next step.

* * *

Getting to this place in my mindset and career didn't happen overnight. For many years I simply worked as a software engineer. I gave no thought to where my career was heading, and even though I always had a strong work ethic and was a talented developer, I never expressed interest in moving up to manager. I considered becoming a professor in the future, or sticking around until I eventually became a software architect. I didn't like the idea of starting over, so I ultimately stayed with the same company in the same position for seven years.

The longer I stayed in the same position, however, the more men I saw advance to team lead. Finally, I decided I wanted to prove that I was capable of doing the same. I talked to my manager, who promised that when a position opened up, it was mine.

But that's not what happened. He gave the team lead role to someone else.

I was so disappointed. My manager had never told me there was an issue with my performance, so I couldn't understand his decision. I asked to be transferred to a different group and immediately told my new manager that I wanted to be team lead.

He hesitated a little and then said, "You are perceived as very aggressive. People are intimidated by you. That's not a good fit for a team lead."

Though his feedback was gendered—a man would be much less likely to hear the same message—it was also true: I was more aggressive than any man I met at work back then. Sharing that information was one of the nicest things anyone has done for me in my career, even though it was hard to hear at the time. Now I knew what I needed to work on if I wanted to be team lead. It wasn't my technical skills; it was a personal blind spot.

It took some time, but I finally showed my manager I could change. He promoted me to team lead, and within a few years, I was managing a project that included thirty people in four countries.

During this time, I got married and my husband and I decided we wanted to have children. This launched us on a complicated and painful journey of fertility treatments, miscarriages, and surrogacy that, thankfully, culminated in the birth of our three children.

Those were dark years. The fertility treatments broke my spirits and greatly affected my hormones, which in turn affected my energy level and mental state.

Because of the emotional difficulties, I struggled to hold a managerial position. After giving birth to my first child, I left high tech and became a personal coach. Interestingly, as I helped others, I grew myself. I spent a great deal of time on personal development: going to therapy, understanding myself better, and working on my blind spots and confidence. Working through these issues was hugely important to me and my growth.

After a year, I realized that I belonged in high tech—and, more specifically, in software engineering. Being far away from coding made me realize how much I missed it. As a result of the personal work I had done, I became less argumentative and insensitive. I learned to put relationships before results, which actually improved results because my team's commitment to me and the company grew in response to the way I treated them.

But I still struggled. I decided to return to my software engineer position because emotionally, I couldn't handle the team lead demands—more one-on-one communication, more patience, more friction, and speaking up when something didn't work—along with the hardship of trying to have another child.

After we discovered that I wasn't able to hold a pregnancy, we searched for a surrogate to carry our second child. We finally found someone through an agency that promised she would be treated fairly, and I felt like a huge weight was lifted off my shoulders. Years and years of failed attempts, miscarriages, hormones, and depression were replaced by hope. I am so grateful for what this woman has given me and my family.

After we found the surrogate, I no longer needed to take hormones. I was able to focus again and my energy returned. I was able to appreciate the way my year in personal coaching had changed me as a person and leader. I was now more focused on the win-win, building a team, and working with people instead of goals and tasks. In short, I was a much better manager.

I also took time to observe the people around me who had advanced to senior executive roles and figure out what they were doing. In particular, I observed the men, because they made up nearly 100 percent of the people advancing in high tech around me. Many of them seemed to share four key attributes:

1. They don't let failure dictate who they are. They shake it off and move on. A few of them even present failures as successes, whether they had missed a due date or received a termination notice.
2. They take every opportunity to advance. They are willing to take a chance at a less successful or less stable company, knowing they can use the experience to look for another position if this company goes under.
3. They don't wait for someone else to tell them they are ready to advance.
4. They don't hesitate when offered a position that is more challenging than what they've done before. They believe they can do it.

Around the same time that I made these observations, I had the revelation mentioned earlier: my career was in *my* hands, not the VP's. Before the VP made a decision about who would advance to a director position, the company underwent a change in management. Despite the upheaval, I stayed and shortly after got promoted. When the VP was replaced with someone I couldn't work for, I took a director position at another organization. When that company closed, I set my sights even higher—I wanted to become vice president, a position I wouldn't have dreamed of pursuing a few years earlier because that option didn't even occur to me. By early 2017, I had achieved this goal. I had gone from software engineer to VP of R&D in less than two years.

This path of advancement on steroids was only possible because I changed my mindset. I reframed my inability to hold the managerial position as an opportunity to go into coaching, learn key managerial skills, and increase my own self-confidence. I put those years of removing myself from leadership behind me, and I moved on. After observing why the men around me were advancing, I started taking more chances, and my fear of failure and not being up for the task disappeared.

* * *

Perhaps you can relate to the early years of my career. Maybe you've been working at the same company, maybe even in the same position, for years, and until recently you've never really thought about what's next. Maybe you've been trying to advance, but so far, you haven't succeeded. Maybe you doubt your ability to handle the work at the next level. Maybe you've faced discrimination or resistance. Maybe you're feeling alone.

I've been there.

I know how it feels to be the only female in the room, to not have a female role model, to realize someone who joined the company after you got promoted to a position you didn't even hear was open. I've managed to climb the ladder in spite of these things, and I can show you the way.

In the past three years I have mentored more than one hundred women in high tech, many of whom are now climbing up the ladder themselves. In this book, I offer the same tips I've shared with them. We'll discuss strategies for:

- Handling problems common to women in many high-tech fields, not just engineering—self-confidence, imposter syndrome, toxic environments, maternity leave, and more.

- Succeeding in your role as a software engineer—looking for a job, relationships with peers and managers, and developing skills so that you stand out.
- Succeeding as a team lead—the new responsibilities you'll face and ways to prepare yourself for the next level.
- Succeeding as a manager—building your manager persona, managing other managers, and handling unique difficulties that arise for women at this level.
- Succeeding as VP of R&D—setting the atmosphere for your organization, understanding where the company is heading, and working with founders and CEOs.

If you want to "woman up" and climb the high-tech ladder, especially if you want to do it quickly, you need to take chances. You need to work on those inner challenges that are holding you back, whether it's lack of confidence or imposter syndrome. You need to be brave.

This world is broken in so many ways. Women and other minorities still experience discrimination in high tech, and as a result, many aspects of our careers are still outside of our control. Still, we can each show up as our best selves and take steps to fix this reality so women in the future do not have to live with it. This book is a guide to help you make the best of the world as it is, to suggest when to fight back and when to leave.

One note: This discussion comes from my own life as a parent in a heterosexual relationship. If you are a single parent, child-free, nonbinary, or a woman in a same-sex relationship, you may not have the same lived experience, but I hope you still find helpful information for your journey up the high-tech ladder.

I am a huge believer in women and their ability to rise up and succeed. I believe women have what it takes to be amazing managers. I can't promise that you won't fail on this journey. This book isn't a magic pill that will automatically guarantee you a senior position. But I can promise you will have the tools to get up and try again.

We'll start by looking at the challenges women experience in tech fields at all levels.

PART I

COMMON PROBLEMS

CHAPTER 1

Obstacles for Women

The above cartoon depicts the experience many women face as they pursue a career in high tech. We are told the race is the same length. We are told to stop complaining. We are told our issues are minor, or that they're figments of our imagination.

Yet our experience tells us something quite different: that the race is not equal, that we face many more obstacles than men, that moving ahead takes much longer.

At every level in high-tech fields, from first-time software engineers to VPs of R&D, women face numerous challenges. In this chapter, we'll discuss the most common obstacles, which tend to fall into four buckets: biological, emotional/psychological, societal/cultural, and environmental/company. Some topics we'll talk about more in later chapters. By looking at these challenges, we can better understand the uphill battle we face as women in high tech.

BIOLOGICAL OBSTACLES

Starting a family is a huge decision that impacts every area of a woman's life, including work. Pregnancy and all that it entails is a biological reality that men don't face, and it can significantly impact a woman's career path. Here's a brief summary of the biological obstacles related to being a woman.

- I've heard people say, "Pregnancy is not a disease, so don't be spoiled." But truthfully, it can be quite difficult. Whether it's struggling to conceive, dealing with at-risk factors, experiencing morning sickness for three or more months, or making time for doctor's appointments, pregnancy takes up a large part of a woman's life. This has a huge impact on a woman's

relationship with work. Men don't experience that difficulty, so they aren't held back by the mental, physical, and emotional drain that comes with pregnancy.
- Even after giving birth, women find work is different. We can experience problems like long hospital stays, hormone changes, or exhaustion from caring for our child that can all affect our ability to perform our jobs. Though their lives will be different after children arrive, men can generally work the same as they did before.
- After the children are born, many mothers like to spend more time at home with their kids. As a result, they might choose a less-interesting job at a less-successful company or take a pay cut to reduce commuting times and be closer to home.

Later in Part I, we'll talk about motherhood, maternity leave, and fertility treatments more directly.

EMOTIONAL AND PSYCHOLOGICAL OBSTACLES

In addition to biological challenges, women face emotional and psychological struggles that statistically don't affect men as much.

- As women, we often are not brave enough to ask for more money, as we can fear appearing greedy. Men don't seem to have the same struggle. Over the course of my career, I have interviewed hundreds of people for software engineer positions. I have seen many women excel in the interview and then ask for so much less money than men who performed less successfully.
- Also related to bravery: research shows that when a woman doesn't fit 100 percent of the requirements for a job posting, she often won't submit her resume. On the other hand, men

will apply for the job even if they only meet 60 percent of the requirements.[1] Men often have the confidence to assume that they can figure out the parts they don't have experience in, whereas women might not feel ready to make those leaps.

- We women often don't experience rejection until we enter the workforce, which makes it more difficult and sometimes shocking when it happens. Men, on the other hand, often experience rejection earlier in life, perhaps because they are expected to be the pursuers in the dating world. As a result, they are usually more accustomed to rejection when it happens in their career and are thus less affected by it.
- As women, we are more likely to experience imposter syndrome. Some studies have suggested men and women experience imposter syndrome in about equal numbers, but new research shows that women indeed suffer from it more frequently.[2]
- Sexual harassment is another potential obstacle that can leave long-term traumatic effects. Even if a woman changes workplaces, harassment can negatively impact her emotional well-being, which can damage her career in the process. Men face sexual harassment at far lower rates. In 2017, for example, men filed only 16.5 percent of the sexual harassment charges received by the Equal Employment Opportunity Commission; the rest were filed by women.[3]

---

[1] Tara Sophia Mohr, "Why Women Don't Apply for Jobs Unless They're 100% Qualified," *Harvard Business Review*, August 25, 2014, https://hbr.org/2014/08/why-women-dont-apply-for-jobs-unless-theyre-100-qualified.

[2] Gina Gibson-Beverly, and Jonathan R. Schwartz, "Attachment, Entitlement, and the Impostor Phenomenon in Female Graduate Students," *Journal of College Counseling* 11, no. 2 (2008), Gale Academic OneFile, https://hbr.org/2014/08/why-women-dont-apply-for-jobs-unless-theyre-100-qualifiedhttps://hbr.org/2014/08/why-women-dont-apply-for-jobs-unless-theyre-100-qualified.

[3] The Women's Initiative, "Gender Matters: Women Disproportionately Report Sexual Harrassment in Male-Dominated Industries," CAP, August 6, 2018, https://www.americanprogress.org/article/gender-matters/.

- Studies have shown that women tend to attribute success to an external factor, but they will blame themselves for any failure.[4]
- From my experience, men are more willing to talk confidently about things they don't know much about. They'll throw buzzwords around and involve themselves in the conversation. Women, on the other hand, tend to wait to speak until they feel confident about the subject matter.

In future chapters we'll discuss ways to build confidence and fight imposter syndrome to help you remove some of these emotional and psychological obstacles.

> **PRO TIP**
>
> Involve yourself in the conversation, even if you're not an expert. Simply mention that you don't know the subject well and then make your contribution. Be involved without pretending to know more than you do.

SOCIETAL AND CULTURAL OBSTACLES

Societal expectations and gender norms often mean that women face more judgment for pursuing a career. The following ideas aren't truth, but rather messages that both boys and girls receive throughout childhood that then become stereotypes about what women should do throughout their adult life.

- As women, we are expected to be caregivers. We are expected to take maternity leave, not just to recover physically but to learn how to care for our children. As time goes on, we con-

---

[4] S. Beyer, "Gender Differences in the Accuracy of Self-Evaluations of Performance," *Journal of Personality and Social Psychology* 59, no. 5 (1990), 960–970. https://doi.org/10.1037/0022-3514.59.5.960.

tinue to become better caregivers, so we do more childcare. Men, on the other hand, are supposed to be providers. They are praised for working long hours in pursuit of a successful career, even if that means less time at home.
- Career-driven women look for successful partners, and we're less focused on whether our husbands can cook or clean or take care of children. This can become an obstacle for our own careers. When we marry someone equally interested in their own career, we have less help around the house than our male coworkers, who may not have married a career-driven woman. Men usually look for a woman who will be a good mother and support their career.
- As women, we are expected to care for the home, as well as the children. Successful men only do about 10 percent of the household work, giving them more time to work long hours and travel for their job. In my own house, where I am the main provider, we end up doing about a sixty-forty split of housework, with my husband handling the bigger percentage. In most cases, the best a successful woman can aim for is a fifty-fifty split of domestic duties.
- Women are expected to follow their husbands for a career opportunity, but the reverse is not as common. Many men aren't willing to follow their wives for a job.[5]
- In general, STEM education favors boys' learning styles over girls. Whether it's programming, math, physics, or other STEM-related fields, schools help boys succeed by focusing on competition, which many boys thrive on, rather than collaborative learning, where girls shine. Not only that, but boys are

---

5 Dina ElBoghdady, "Why Couples Move for a Man's Job, but Not a Woman's," *Washington Post*, November 28, 2014, https://www.washingtonpost.com/news/wonk/wp/2014/11/28/why-couples-move-for-a-mans-job-but-not-a-womans/; Alan Benson, "Re-Thinking the Two-Body Problem: The Segregation of Women into Geographically Dispersed Occupations," *Demography* 41, no. 4 (2013), http://dx.doi.org/10.2139/ssrn.1925913.

expected to succeed in these areas, so they are more likely to rise to that standard, but even low-achieving boys are encouraged to pursue STEM more than most girls.[6] In one study, boys and girls were separated into different classrooms. The girls did better at math when boys were not in their classrooms, partly because they were able to ask the questions they needed to ask without feeling ashamed.[7]

- The stereotype that STEM is for boys discourages many girls from pursuing it in coed classrooms.[8] This stereotype is reinforced by the fact that girls don't see many women teaching STEM classes. Seeing female role models in STEM can help girls choose this path because they see possible career choices. Research also shows that grade bias happens against girls: there's evidence that if teachers see a girl's name on a test, they will give her a lower grade for the same work. Additionally, parents' bias can discourage girls from pursuing math and other STEM courses.[9] Girls are just as capable, but they have to be given the chance first.

- A similar "grading bias" is seen in the workplace too. In one study, employers were handed many resumes. The pile included two identical resumes: one from a man, the other

---

6 Victor Lavy and Edith Sand, "On The Origins of Gender Human Capital Gaps: Short and Long Term Consequences of Teachers' Stereotypical Biases," *National Bureau of Economic Research*, January 2015, https://www.nber.org/papers/w20909; Sarah D. Sparks, "Low-Achieving Boys Opt for STEM Careers More Than Most Girls Do," *EducationWeek*, June 26, 2020, https://www.edweek.org/teaching-learning/low-achieving-boys-opt-for-stem-careers-more-than-most-girls-do/2020/06.

7 Michael Gurian, Kathy Stevens, and Peggy Daniels, "Single-Sex Classrooms Are Succeeding," Educational Horizons 87, no. 4 (2009): 234-45, http://www.jstor.org/stable/42923774; Heather Blair and Kathy Sanford, "Single-Sex Classrooms: A Place for Transformation of Policy and Practice," University of Alberta Canada, (April 1999), https://eric.ed.gov/?id=ED433285.

8 R.E. O'Dea et al., "Gender differences in individual variation in academic grades fail to fit expected patterns for STEM," Nat Commun 9, 3777, 2018, https://doi.org/10.1038/s41467-018-06292-0.

9 Selina McCoy, Delma Byrne, and Pat O Connor, "Gender Stereotyping in Parents' and Teachers' Perceptions of Boys' and Girls' Mathematics Performance in Ireland," Working Papers 202010, Geary Institute, University College Dublin, 2020, https://ideas.repec.org/p/ucd/wpaper/202010.html.

from a woman. When researchers asked the employer how much he would pay each candidate, he offered the woman a lot less than the man even though they had the *same* resume.[10]

- We can also get in our own way. Because of gender norms, we might tell ourselves, "I'm better at taking care of the kids," or "My husband doesn't know how to take care of them." We might doubt that he's responsible enough. The truth is, men can be caregivers. Many women don't see this until after they divorce. Then they see that their ex can maintain a home and care for the children.

In high school, I chose to take a math and programming class. It had three girls and thirty boys. Looking back, I have to ask why the gender gap was already so transparent. We were less than 10 percent of the class. We were already the minority in *high school*. It could be that girls have less interest in those subjects. It could be a lack of role models. Or it could be the result of societal expectations impressed on girls from a young age.

> **PRO TIP**
>
> If you want a successful career, don't lower your expectations for your husband. Don't let them skip taking care of their own children. Believe that they can put in the work at home. Doing so will allow you to focus more on your career and possibly save your marriage.

---

[10] Judd B. Kessler, Corinne Low, and Colin D. Sullivan, "Incentivized Resume Rating: Eliciting Employer Preferences without Deception," University of Pennsylvania (February 2019), https://faculty.wharton.upenn.edu/wp-content/uploads/2018/09/KesslerLowSullivan_Revision1.pdf; Corinne A. Moss-Racusin et al., "Science Faculty's Subtle Gender Biases Favor Male Students," Proceedings of the National Academy of Sciences 109, no. 41 (October 9, 2012), https://www.pnas.org/doi/10.1073/pnas.1211286109.

ENVIRONMENTAL AND WORKPLACE OBSTACLES

Work environments bring their own set of challenges. Women must navigate issues like bias and lack of role models, in addition to learning skills to help them climb the ladder.

- Often, women don't have female role models to show us how to succeed in our companies. For example, early in my career, I wanted to be a successful manager but was seen as too aggressive. I didn't have someone to show me how to be assertive but not aggressive. I had to learn how to do it on my own.
- Likewise, many women are turned off from a company if there aren't women already there. Being the only one can be lonely. This isn't true of everyone, but many women don't want to join a team as the only female, which can limit their opportunities.
- Because of the gender gap in engineering, women are less likely to have female mentorship, which can make it harder to rise within a company. Men, on the other hand, have plenty of mentors available. In Israel, men make up the majority of technology units in the army, and some women choose to leave those units as a result. Even if they stay, many find it is harder to network and use those connections outside of the army when they start their careers.
- Many women face employer discrimination. Often, employers don't expect women to want things like promotions, so they pass over them. This goes hand in hand with mentorship: men often take other men under their wing and help them climb the ladder at work. Mentors can support their mentees, tell them about opportunities, and coach them to succeed. They also teach people how to behave to fit into that company's environment.
- Within a company, men and women are also often given different labels for the same behavior. Whereas men might be

labeled great decision makers if they are assertive, women are often seen as aggressive. Whereas men might be praised for asking for what they need to reach their goal, women would be labeled demanding or bitchy.[11] Someone told me that when her male coworkers became aggressive at work, they sometimes pounded tables with their fists. She pointed out that she couldn't behave like that and be taken seriously.

- Along with the labels, women often receive mixed messages about how to behave. If we ask for something a couple of times, we're seen as nagging, but if we relax and things fall between the cracks, we're blamed. If we're too assertive, we're called a bitch. If we aren't assertive enough, we're seen as weak.
- Women are usually offered less money for the same position and experience. Depending on the position, women earn 60 to 80 percent of what their male counterparts do.
- Even when companies post jobs, their wording is often geared toward men. They might say they're looking for an "engineering ninja" or "frontend rockstar" or "data science superstar." Because women are less likely to identify with these words, we are less likely to apply.
- Toxic environments can affect everyone, but some impact women more significantly. For example, I know someone who was the only woman in an engineering department. The men often made sexual jokes, so she went to HR. They told her not to worry. Boys will be boys. Don't take it so seriously. It was only after she went to a senior manager that the situation was handled. Some women feel they must leave their job because of how negatively it affects their mental and emotional well-being.

---

[11] Victoria L. Brescoll and Eric Uhlmann, "Can an Angry Woman Get Ahead? Status Conferral, Gender, and Expression of Emotion in the Workplace," *Psychological Science* 19, no. 3 (2008): 268–275, https://journals.sagepub.com/doi/full/10.1111/j.1467-9280.2008.02079.x

- Many women feel ignored in meetings. When women speak up, our comments are ignored or interrupted. Additionally, men will sometimes make the same point and then be praised for saying what we've already said. I've read countless testimonials about women not being heard at work.
- Work dynamics can be tricky, even with feminist men. New research finds that 60 percent of male managers are uncomfortable mentoring or working with women.[12] Men sometimes distance themselves from their female coworkers and employees, not because they doubt their abilities, but because they fear how it looks. Sometimes they even worry about how it looks to women themselves. This again leads to women having fewer mentors and opportunities.

> **PRO TIP**
>
> Women can be easily influenced by criticism, so mixed messaging can lead to confusion and getting stuck. My advice? Be the person you choose to be. For example, be assertive and in the details, if that suits you, and be prepared for criticism.

It can be exhausting to talk with male coworkers about discrimination in the workplace. It's hard to talk about toxic work environments without sounding bitter or unhappy. Often, men think the discrimination isn't real. They point out that women go to work. Women have careers. Women wear what they want and vote in elections. So the age of discrimination must be over.

---

[12] "Men, Commit to Mentor Women," LeanIn.org, https://leanin.org/mentor-her#!.

But that's not true. Women don't discuss it because it's exhausting to talk about the reality and be ignored.

WHAT'S NEXT?

Yes, a career in high-tech is full of obstacles, but don't let that stop you. Our discussion here is just to show you what might lie ahead, not to discourage you from pursuing your career. You can succeed in your field. It involves hard work, but you can do it.

The next two chapters will look more closely at two big issues in the emotional and psychological bucket: self-confidence and imposter syndrome.

CHAPTER 2

Self-Confidence

I used to hate interviews; they really scared me. To help me get through them with less fear, I started picturing the way one of my colleagues handled interviews and pressure in general. I thought about how he responded to questions he didn't know the answer to, how he stayed calm even when he felt like the interview wasn't going well, and how he stayed positive and poised even when he felt he was being treated poorly. I'd mentally go through the whole interview at home, imagining myself displaying that same cool demeanor.

After much practice, both on my own and in actual interviews, I became more confident and my fear went away.

Self-confidence is an essential inner quality in any career, but especially as a woman in high tech where your abilities might be questioned before you even start your role, just because you're a woman. This chapter will discuss how to build self-confidence and fake it until you become more brave.

THE IMPORTANCE OF SELF-CONFIDENCE

Everyone experiences a lack of self-confidence now and then, but for the sake of your career, it's important to consciously work on this trait. Self-confidence leads to better performance, as well as good feelings about yourself and what you can achieve. Overcoming self-doubts happens when you honestly and truthfully assess your abilities and work on areas that need improvement.

When you lack self-confidence, you can fall into some traps that can hold you back. For example, when you're a junior and learning at a company, you might get into the habit of taking the blame when things go wrong. As a result, you can start thinking you're stupid or not capable of handling this position. But it's not on you. You're not supposed to understand everything from the beginning.

A lack of self-confidence can also lead you to be too modest and hide your success or to let someone else take credit. You might think that your managers will see what you're doing and promote you without you speaking up, but it usually doesn't work that way. You might feel too shy to do your own PR and hope a coworker will notice and spread the word. You can't rely on that either. If you aren't naturally confident, you need to fake it, share your successes, and do your own PR.

At the same time, self-confidence doesn't mean thinking you never make mistakes. Everyone does, no matter how confident they are or how long they've been in their career. Don't get stuck on being perfect. Remember: better done than perfect.

BUILDING SELF-CONFIDENCE

The most important thing I have done for my career is building my self-confidence, and lack of confidence is the number one issue I see in the women I mentor. The good news is that self-confidence can be learned. Here are ten tips to get you started:

1. **Intentionally work on building self-confidence by reading a self-help book or by getting help from another person.** Find a therapist to analyze your negative patterns. Get a coach to help you practice being brave. Find what triggers your lack of confidence and the beliefs that limit you. For example, you might think, "I am not smart enough," "Everyone knows that I am not technical," or "I didn't finish my feature on time so I am a bad developer." Once you recognize these thought patterns, you can work through them in therapy, coaching, or speaking with other women. Stop yourself when you notice these negative thoughts, and ask yourself what you would tell a friend who spoke to herself in this harsh way. Also, look at the things you say to yourself and evaluate whether or not they're true. Maybe you tell yourself you're a bad developer, but when you reflect, you realize you deliver good features consistently. If it helps, write down the truth about your skills so you remember next time self-doubt creeps in.
2. **Try things you don't think you can do.** Start a technological blog. Give a lecture. Present at a conference. Try something that is harder than your current skill level. You might think something like speaking at a conference takes a lot of self-confidence, but it's really a matter of preparation and practice. Building diverse professional skills is one of the best ways to build confidence in your abilities. The more you do it, the more your confidence will grow.
3. **Engage in meetings even when you don't feel 100 percent sure about the topic.** Ask questions. Share your perspective. The more you do it, the more confident you'll become.

4. **Even if you fail when you take a risk, learn from that experience.** Separate yourself from failure. You did something, and it failed. You are not a failure. Learn from the situation and then move on.
5. **Believe you're worthy of a promotion.** Aim high. Ask yourself what you need to do to make it to that next position. Look at the steps and start taking them.
6. **Look for a supportive community.** Within your team, find a buddy, someone you can learn from in those areas where your current knowledge and skills are limited.
7. **Ask people who appreciate you to encourage you.** Find people who can help you calm down when you're feeling nervous, like before a big presentation. When you share how you're feeling, these friends can show you how valuable you truly are.
8. **Change your goals.** If you're scared about finding a new job, change the goal from "finding a new job" to "getting as many interviews as possible." If you succeed in getting interviews, then you've already won. Eventually you will get a job.
9. **If you have a huge task, break it down to small tasks.** Small steps are usually easier to handle, practically and emotionally, and little wins can boost your confidence.
10. **When you're scared, imagine someone who has confidence—** just as I did when I was scared to interview. Imagine this person doing what you need to do. How does she handle herself? How does she speak? Notice the small details and then try to imitate them in your own situation.

In general, women hold themselves back because of internal obstacles like low self-confidence. Men are better at preserving their inner strength: even if they fail again and again, men keep their confidence. By intentionally working on your own confidence, you can do the same.

FAKE IT TILL YOU MAKE IT

Here's a mantra to remember when it comes to building self-confidence: fake it till you make it. Give that presentation. Ask that question. Participate in that discussion. Make your voice heard even if you're trembling inside. Don't wait until you have confidence to do big, meaningful things. Instead, set big goals and work toward them. This will build your confidence.

Many women with low self-confidence struggle with imposter syndrome. Our next chapter will look at this syndrome and how to overcome it.

CHAPTER 3

Imposter Syndrome

Lia was working as a senior software engineer in a medium-sized company where she was loved and appreciated. Due to her excellent work, Lia was in a secure position within the company.[13]

Eventually, a new senior named Nathan joined the team, and they worked parallel to each other. Lia told him everything she knew and helped him with his onboarding. They seemed to have a good working relationship.

After a while, Lia noticed that Nathan was very harsh with her code reviews. He insisted on a code style of his own, which was not a part of the team's guidelines. When he didn't like her solutions, he insisted she replace them, even though she had logical reasons for the way she implemented her feature. If she didn't agree with him, he would argue and then send her multiple follow-up emails, which drove her crazy.

---

13 In all of the stories shared in this book, names have been changed. However, I've used the real names of the women highlighted in the "In Her Words" sidebars.

While she knew that she had sound logic, Lia kept giving in to her imposter syndrome and Nathan's pestering because she felt intimidated. Because of his behavior, Lia forgot she was an excellent developer and doubted herself constantly. She forgot she deserved seniority in the team, and that she and Nathan were equals. She came to me feeling frustrated and was considering leaving her workplace because of Nathan.

Lia and I talked about ways for her to find inner strength again. I helped her remember how much she knew within high tech and we talked through actions she could take at work.

She started by establishing boundaries with Nathan and stopped letting him nag her endlessly. When he pressed her, she'd reply, "I heard you. My professional opinion is different, and I don't want to continue this discussion anymore."

To solve his constant critique of her coding style, Lia asked her team lead about setting up formal code review guidelines. That way Nathan couldn't keep taking issue with her style if it matched the team's outline. I also suggested involving her team lead, but Lia felt it would make her look childish and incapable of handling her own problems. I respected that.

After we talked, things got better for Lia. Some of the nagging continued, but remembering how imposter syndrome affected her confidence, she kept reminding herself of her abilities, which reduced his effect on her.

This chapter will define imposter syndrome and provide solutions for working through it.

WHAT IS IMPOSTER SYNDROME?

Imposter syndrome is a psychological pattern where people doubt their achievements and worry constantly that they'll be exposed as imposters. It can be accompanied by anxiety, stress, rumination, or depression. The term was coined in 1978 by two clinical psychologists, Pauline Rose Clance and Suzanne Imes, after conducting research surrounding women and their self-perceived performance compared to how they were actually doing at work.

People with this syndrome are generally successful. Despite this, they feel like frauds. They feel like they don't deserve their success and that it was actually the result of good luck or timing. They don't think of themselves as intelligent or capable. They believe people will find out they're not as gifted and talented as they appear. None of these beliefs constitute reality.

At first, researchers thought imposter syndrome only affected women, but both men and women have it.[14] Still, it is very common among women: according to a study released by KPMG in 2020, 75 percent of women in managerial positions experience imposter syndrome.

Imposter syndrome often comes from perfectionism, self-doubt, fear of failure, or anxiety. Since women are often harder on themselves than men, it makes sense that they experience imposter syndrome more often. They tell themselves that they're not good enough, and this voice is often much stronger than the voice telling them they *are* good enough. Because this negative self-talk lowers self-esteem, women with imposter syndrome sometimes

---

14 Joe Langford and Pauline Rose Clance, "The Impostor Phenomenon: Recent Research Findings Regarding Dynamics, Personality and Family Patterns and Their Implications for Treatment," *Psychotherapy: Theory, Research, Practice, Training* 30, no. 3 (Fall 1993): 495–501, doi:10.1037/0033-3204.30.3.495.

rethink their career choice because they don't think they can handle the one they really want.

This syndrome is damaging. It prevents us from speaking up in meetings and asking for raises. It causes us to focus on staying under the radar or working overtime to prove to *ourselves* that we are good enough. It causes us stress and anxiety.

Though men and women both experience imposter syndrome, bias and exclusion in the workplace can exacerbate the feelings of doubt felt by women and further influence their ability to succeed. As mentioned earlier, the world is not perfect or fair. These outside conditions may not change in your lifetime. But you can take these feelings and this reality and transform them into positive motivation.

Whether or not your imposter syndrome is made worse by a biased work environment, you can take steps to overcome it.

OVERCOMING IMPOSTER SYNDROME

So how do you overcome this negative self-talk?

First, you must normalize it. Remind yourself that a lot of women have it. In many ways, imposter syndrome is similar to self-confidence, so go back and review the tips for building confidence. The two internal struggles really go hand in hand. As you build confidence, your battle with imposter syndrome will likely decrease.

You also need to normalize failure. It happens to everyone. If you have imposter syndrome, failure feels like the worst thing that could ever happen and it fills you with guilt and shame. If you normalize failure, you'll see it as part of life, that failing at a task doesn't make you a failure. You can fail, and everything will be fine.

Just as you are ready to fail, so to speak, be ready to succeed. Celebrate it. Don't reject it and say you don't deserve it or it's by chance.

I also suggest that you find different sources of encouragement. Ask your friends what they think of you. Talk to a mentor. Be your own cheerleader, not your own enemy.

Also, know your own worth and don't compare yourself to others. In Hebrew we say, "Have your own backbone." It comes from a term about not having a backbone, or being spineless and weak. The opposite of being spineless is knowing who you are and standing up for yourself—your worth, your opinions, your abilities, your achievements.

When you have imposter syndrome, you tell yourself stories that *aren't* true. To overcome this, write out all of the stories you tell yourself and fact-check them. Ask a trusted friend to look at your list and tell you if they see any truth.

Failure is a part of life, but when you succeed, enjoy it. Have a healthy approach to both failure and success, and your imposter syndrome will start fading away.

Because they often struggle with self-confidence and imposter syndrome, many women have a hard time asking for the salary they deserve. We'll cover that next.

CHAPTER 4

Negotiating Salary

When mentees are job hunting and ask me about salaries, I always give them the same advice: research the salary range for your skill level and expertise. When they do, they can't believe what they find. "Those numbers can't be true!" they tell me.

"Go ask your male peers from university what they are making," I then suggest.

At that point my mentees can't deny the numbers. They realize that the going salary for men is up to 40 percent more than they intended to ask.

As women, we often struggle with asking for a raise or negotiating a salary. This chapter will look at why it can be harder for us, as well as how you can get the salary you deserve.

THE SITUATION

Here's the situation: women earn less than men in every industry, including in high tech. According to the Bureau of Labor Statistics, we earn on average eighty-two cents for every dollar a man earns. At every level of education, women earn less than men, and the gap is most apparent among women of color: black and Latina women earn 65 percent of what white men do when they both hold bachelor's degrees.[15] Not only that, but studies have shown that the pay gap is *increasing* in the tech industry; one study first conducted in 2015 found that women in San Jose earned 86.4 percent of what men made. In 2021, that same study found women only made 81 percent of what men made.[16] That means you almost certainly earn less than the guy sitting next to you.

There are many reasons for this wage gap. For one, women are socialized to not ask for things upfront, so we often don't negotiate for more money when we are hired or ask for raises before they are offered.[17] When that's stacked on top of the fact that we're probably offered less to begin with, the gap increases. Even if we ask for the same salary as men, research shows that we still get less.[18]

Some women compromise on salary because of children. We want to work fewer hours, which might translate to asking for a lower salary because we know we won't be at the office as much as is

---

15 Janelle Jones, "5 Facts About the State of the Gender Pay Gap," *U.S. Department of Labor Blog*, March 19, 2021, https://blog.dol.gov/2021/03/19/5-facts-about-the-state-of-the-gender-pay-gap.

16 Grace Stetson, "Report: The Tech Industry Gender Pay Gap in San Jose Has Grown," *San Jose Inside*, February 26, 2021, https://www.sanjoseinside.com/news/report-the-tech-industry-gender-pay-gap-in-san-jose-has-grown/.

17 Emily T Amanatullah and Michael W Morris, "Negotiating gender roles: gender differences in assertive negotiating are mediated by women's fear of backlash and attenuated when negotiating on behalf of others," *J Pers Soc Psychol*, February 2010, https://pubmed.ncbi.nlm.nih.gov/20085399/.

18 Daniel Victor, "Research Suggests Women Are Asking for Raises, But Men Get Them More," The New York Times, September 6, 2016, https://www.nytimes.com/2016/09/07/business/research-suggests-women-are-asking-for-raises-but-men-get-them-more.html.

expected. As discussed, some of us lack confidence. We doubt ourselves and our abilities and forget that employers actually want us to work for them, so we don't ask for what our skills are worth. Some of us have a problematic relationship with money to begin with. We view money as dirty or don't believe we deserve it, or we simply don't want to talk about it. Plus, we don't want to be perceived as greedy. Stereotypically, men take care of finances, and studies have shown that women asking for money are often perceived as problematic.

> **PRO TIP**
>
> Remember: companies *want* you to work for them; they're not hiring you as a personal favor. They value your skills, think you can contribute to their organization, and are willing to pay you a fair salary. You don't have to agree to the first offer you're given. You are free to negotiate.

Once you become aware of the gap, you can do something about it. For example, if you see something in yourself that is holding you back from asking for a raise or simply talking about money, talk with someone about it, whether a coach or a good friend. You can also practice asking for a raise. As you become more comfortable doing this, your confidence will also increase.

In addition, look for women around you—your friends, for example—who earn close to or equal what the men do and find out what they do differently. You'll probably learn that they figured out how to earn respect within the company, perhaps through more hours or working effectively. They might know how to market themselves, and they have most likely grown in self-confidence.

They know what they're worth and that they deserve to earn the same as their male colleagues.

HOW TO NEGOTIATE

Even if money is a difficult topic for you to discuss, you can learn how to ask for what you deserve. The following tips will work whether you're negotiating a salary for a new role at a different company or asking for a raise in your current job.

KNOW YOUR VALUE

Some women have trouble marketing themselves, either because they lack confidence or are afraid of being seen as vain. If you're asking for a raise or a certain salary, however, you don't have a choice.

As a reminder of your worth, keep track of the value you have brought to different roles: projects you've completed, processes you've improved, ways you've succeeded, how you've helped your colleagues grow, how you've grown, your strengths, your contributions, and more. Keep a list of references as well, people who can attest to your value. Bring these examples with you to the negotiating table and let them speak for themselves.

> **PRO TIP**
>
> As part of negotiating for a raise, you can also mention other offers if you have them. Don't make it sound like a threat. Mention how much you enjoy working there. You don't want to make it seem like you only care about money, but you also want to get what you're worth.

RESEARCH YOUR RANGE

As mentioned earlier, I give this advice to all of my mentees: learn how much someone with your knowledge and experience makes. In Israel, agencies and companies create charts with this information, and that's likely true wherever you live. Plus, you can always look online. If you want a point of comparison that's closer to home, ask your male colleagues what they're earning.

ASK HIGH

After you understand the range, ask at the high end. In fact, I recommend asking for 10 percent more than the number you have in mind. It's not a lot more; it doesn't make you sound greedy. And asking for more leaves room for negotiation. Usually, employers won't stop the hiring process if you ask higher than they want to give. They might say they can't pay that, but the lower number they offer is often still higher than what you originally had in mind. I have seen many success stories when women asked high.

PRACTICE BEFOREHAND

Prepare for your negotiation by rehearsing it with someone—a friend who's succeeded at getting raises or old work colleagues who hold the same position as you. Know what you're going to say. Prepare how you'll present yourself; ideally, you want to come across as pleasant and confident.

It can be especially helpful to brainstorm problems that can come up in the discussion and how you would handle each scenario. For example, you might ask for a raise and be met with an immediate no. If this happens, remind them of your accomplishments and success. List features you've worked on that performed well, people you onboarded, and initiations you had. If you're continually met with a no, ask for a date when a raise is possible or ask for a bonus instead. If their response is that they don't see a raise in the future for you, consider if it's worthwhile to stay at that company.

You might also face a situation where you're told you aren't experienced enough to ask for that amount of money. Prepare for this by checking the numbers beforehand, and be ready to provide them with proof that your ask is reasonable based on your experience and any other added value you bring to the table.

Have your friend or coworker challenge you with these different reactions and comments so you can practice giving a calm, well-worded response.

TAKE YOUR TIME

Once a potential employer makes an offer, thank them and ask for time to think. There's no reason to accept immediately. *Always* go home and think about it, consult with friends—especially ones who are paid highly—and prepare your response.

If you received the offer you wanted, then there's not much to practice in terms of your response. You should still ensure that the rest of the terms are solid—days off, RSU (restricted stock unit), options, and bonuses, for example. While this might feel greedy, I've seen men negotiating for these aspects of their contract, so feel empowered to do the same.

If you didn't get the offer you wanted, you'll want to start with good reasons why you should get the salary you asked for. For example, you can say, "I really want the position, but I don't feel comfortable with this offer. It's too low." You can also bring up your relevant experience and other higher offers you've received, as well as your amazing record and impressive recommendations.

And remember: the employer wants you. You have power in this situation. Take your time and negotiate to get the salary you want and deserve.

IT'S MORE THAN MONEY

Let's say you are at a dead end in your salary talks but you really want the job. Try negotiating benefits like days off, annual bonuses, sign-on bonuses, and shares in the company, all of which are worth money. Start with what matters to you; if you like taking long vacations, pursue days off first. Likewise, if you believe in the company, push for shares and options. If you're in a tight place financially at the moment, push for a sign-on bonus.

MAKE SPACE FOR GROWTH

If you agree on a lower salary than your target number, ask the employer to state in the contract that your salary will grow. Make sure the wording includes specific numbers—a percentage or a dollar amount increase—and a timeline.

The same is true if you ask for a raise. Sometimes the employer can't give you an increase right now, but later it will be possible. Ask for a written agreement, even in email, that states the date you will get a raise and how much.

DON'T APOLOGIZE

In your negotiations, particularly with a new employer, you might come across questions that are dismissive of your abilities or the hours you can work as a mother. These might be anywhere from, "How will you manage the hours?" to "Who will stay home with your children when they're sick?" Be ready with answers, whether that means repeating your accomplishments or emphasizing what you can achieve. Practice delivering your responses in a pleasant way that doesn't leave room for discussion.

It's not legal for an employer to ask about your status as a mom, for example, whether you plan on getting pregnant in the next two years, nor is it legal for them to ask how your responsibilities as a mother will affect your ability to do your job, but employers might do it anyway. If they bring it up, repeat your experience, your successes, your accomplishments, and so on. Show them that you have already proven you can do the work and can succeed in the position. At the same time, if an employer asks these kinds of questions, you might consider whether that's a place you really want to work.

Don't ever apologize for who and what you are. Remember your value. Remember that you are most likely being paid less than the guy sitting next to you. Remember that people want to hire you. Go into your next salary negotiation with confidence and ask for what you deserve.

CHAPTER 5

Building a Support Network

Picture this: You're in a work meeting. There are ten of you sitting around a table: eight men and two women. When you speak, you are often interrupted by one of the men. At one point, the guy across from you shares an idea that is actually yours. You just mentioned it ten minutes ago. Later, two of the guys get into a heated discussion about the expected scale of your production. One slams the table every time he makes a point, and the other raises his voice until he's almost shouting. They dominate the space in a way you and your female colleague don't feel comfortable doing.

Sound familiar? If you haven't experienced this yourself, you can probably imagine how frustrating it would be.

Meetings like this are just one of the ways that the workplace can be very difficult for us women, and they are one of many reasons we need a support system. This chapter discusses the types of support available and the benefits to you and your career.

INTERNAL SUPPORT

The first place to look for support is inside your company, since this is the most easily accessible. Your support system might consist of a small group of women, for example, three or four team leads, or it might be you and one colleague. No matter how many women are involved, it's a good idea to meet every few weeks so you can regularly touch base, raise dilemmas, brainstorm solutions, share experiences, and offer advice.

One way to actively offer support is to stand up for each other in meetings. Think back to the scenario at the beginning of the chapter. In a meeting like that where men keep cutting off one of the women, her female colleague could speak up and say something like, "I want Sarah to finish her point. I didn't hear everything." Or if someone tried to take credit for Sarah's point, the other woman could say, "Yes, Sarah just said that. It's a great point." In this way, you can help each other be heard and have your ideas acknowledged.

Having someone to bond with inside the company is ideal. Then you can go to lunch more often and discuss the problems you're each experiencing. Ideally, try to organize a weekly or monthly meeting among interested women. It can be fairly informal, but having a designated time to meet can help make sure it actually happens.

If you don't have someone to talk to internally, you can seek support outside of work.

EXTERNAL SUPPORT

In Israel, there are a number of communities that provide external support to women in tech.

Baot (baot.org) is Israel's largest community of women software engineers, doctors, scientists, and researchers. Their mission is to help members create meaningful careers and thrive at work. They're also working to solve the "leaky pipeline" of women leaving high tech. Women end up leaving the field for a variety of reasons, including feeling alone, being targets of harassment and sexism, and disliking the pressures of a male-dominated field. According to the *Harvard Business Review*, 41 percent of women working in tech end up leaving the field compared to just 17 percent of men.[19]

Along with working to solve the leaky pipeline problem, Baot provides ample resources to support women in their careers. They host forums for CTOs, VPs, tech leaders, and architects. They also provide training in finding a job, improving interview skills, writing tech blogs, and building projects such as a technical project code with a professional mentor. They also promote female figures in tech conferences.

In addition, Baot holds groups called Workspace Intelligence, where women discuss challenges in the workplace and find effective solutions. I joined one of these groups and found it very helpful. I met amazing women, extended my network, heard that others were going through similar problems to my own, and helped a few women with their own problems. Overall, it gave me a sense of community.

---

19 Joan C. Williams, "Hacking Tech's Diversity Problem," *Harvard Business Review*, October 2014, https://hbr.org/2014/10/hacking-techs-diversity-problem.

> **PRO TIP**
>
> Let's say you start your own group. What should you talk about when you meet? I say, let the group raise the topics. Then you can see what bothers other women. You can also take some of the topics in this book—asking for a raise, maternity leave, dealing with toxic environments—and use them as a starting point in your discussions.

When it comes to maternity leave, Baot helps women keep their position at their company, along with hosting meetings among mothers in high tech. Those meetings provide a support network, allowing mothers to meet other women in their position, as well as a place to ask for support and advice.

The second big support group, *Women in Tech Israel*, was founded in 2017 to support women working in all high-tech careers, not just software engineering. This innovative and unique community focuses on providing support, encouragement, and mutual help, as well as raising awareness of gender biases and providing tools for career development. As of this writing, there are 15,000 members.

Women in Tech Israel focuses on mentorship, women on maternity leave, and monthly build-yourself-up events. Through their activities and tools, Women in Tech Israel teaches women to take responsibility for their careers, to negotiate salaries, what questions to ask before accepting a new job, how to stand out in meetings, and more. They teach women not to be afraid to report sexual harassment or to have a conversation about pregnancy, maternity leave, or having children. They encourage women to select the right job, leave if they're in the wrong one, and dare to ask for a promotion when it's time. They teach the importance of work-life balance, and to dream big on all the opportunities that are out there. Their goal is to drive women to make a change in their lives and their workplace.

Both Baot and Women in Tech Israel started on Facebook, but they became so successful that women started to volunteer to give lectures in meetups. So it's not always even the leaders of the groups; women inside the group will start things too. When the community is strong, initiative will happen. These groups are really inspirational and the leaders work really hard for other women.

After years of mentoring women from Baot informally, I started a mentoring program in Baot. I help match mentors with mentees and support mentors with any questions or concerns they may have.

To find a similar group, search for "women in tech" in your area. Look for a group in your specific field or for high tech in general. If there isn't one, start it yourself.

THE IMPORTANCE OF COMMUNITY

The early years of my career were really lonely. I didn't see any women in engineering and almost no women in management, so I didn't have anyone to talk to about the struggles I was having as a woman. The women I mentor say they see plenty of brave men, but very few courageous women. Female support systems inside and outside your organization can meet both of these needs. They can ease your sense of being alone and provide you with people who understand the obstacles you're facing, and they can also provide strong, competent role models. It's inspiring to meet charismatic women who write technical blogs and speak at tech conferences, women just like you who are doing things you may not have thought possible.

If you don't have a support system, start one. We are all different, yet many of our dilemmas are the same and we can handle them better together. Communities strengthen us and inspire us to be our best selves. They give us the courage to tackle complicated and difficult challenges. One such challenge that many women encounter is toxic work environments, which we cover next.

IN HER WORDS: DALYA GARTZMAN

I don't feel comfortable in my comfort zone. Come to think of it, I'm not sure I ever had a comfort zone.

I remember as a kid hearing something about people being bored sometimes. I never got that. Whenever I got bored, I just found something else to do. Of course, not all of my teachers liked what I chose to do, but I had good grades, so no one really cared. The other kids surely didn't like my choices, and I was the class's outcast for most of the primary school.

Luckily, I grew up before ADHD was a thing, so I didn't have to numb through boring classes.

Luckily, I went to university when ADHD was very much a thing, and I could easily get medication, or else an MSc. in Math would not have happened.

But an MSc. in Math did happen. Actually, when the time finally came to focus on a subject for my thesis in Math, I decided to pursue a thesis in Computational Biology instead. And this was a time when I knew nothing about computers or biology. Talk about imposter syndrome? I *was* an imposter.

That's how at the age of thirty I started coding for the first time.

And I loved it.

I loved applying my theoretical and mathematical education and creating something tangible. I loved the logic, the order, the structure. It became clear to me how code and algorithms are the natural extensions of the language of math.

That's how I learned lesson 1: Making giant leaps out of your comfort zone leads to gigantic growth.

Right around that time, I also discovered I was a woman. I mean, I always knew that at some level, but I was wild like the boys, smart like the boys, independent like the boys, so how come I was a girl? And more importantly, I wondered, are there more women like me out there? Am I actually wild, smart, and independent like the girls?

Feminism came to my doorstep (as in, my social media feed): Beyoncé said, "I'm not Bossy, I'm the Boss"; Sheryl Sandberg said, "Don't leave before you leave"; and Marissa Mayer didn't even leave for that long anyway. I had so many new possibilities!

Sheryl Sandberg also asked, "What would you do if you weren't afraid?" and I answered, "try and have a meaningful career, I guess?" That's how at the age of thirty-three, when all my friends had already advanced in their careers, I was looking for a "grown-up" job for the first time.

And no one returned my emails.

So I studied some more. I took online classes, went to meetups, and discovered the high-tech industry is not at all gray and dull but is actually fascinating and friendly. I spent two months on a challenging hands-on project and gave a talk at a meetup about this project.

The proactive approach I took to my professional development helped me look better on my resume, and I made connections that benefited my job search.

And then. Finally! I started getting interviews. It took me six months from the moment I started looking for a job until I found what was then my dream job: developing algorithms for an established and exciting startup.

That's how I learned lesson 2: It's never too late to start anything.

My first year as an algorithms developer felt like I was flying at light speed.

I talked at conferences about novel algorithms I developed, organized meetups, and even founded a successful meetup for my professional niche. I was wholly immersed in Baot, mentoring women from across the industry, and I even had a majority of women speakers in my events. I also started a tech blog and was probably juggling more extracurricular activities than I can remember. I didn't go to the beach as much as I wanted, though, so not all was perfect.

Sadly, all these grand aspirations did not sit well with my position, and I felt my cue to look for bigger shoes to fill. After just over a year, I was ready to make another leap.

I left my job without knowing what was next, but I was glad to discover that all the connections I made through my extracurricular activities led to a busy schedule with opportunities.

That's how I learned lesson 3: Your professional karma is the engine that drives your career. Help your peers, share your knowledge, and good things will come your way.

Nonetheless, looking for a job is hard! The emotional roller coaster proved to be quite challenging. I know they say, "If you get only *yeses* it means you're aiming too low," and heck did I get my share of *noes*. In addition, I was keen on avoiding the same mistakes—this time, I was looking for the biggest shoes I could find.

That's how I learned lesson 4: When looking for a job, focus on your personal and professional growth, so that as time goes by, you can aim even higher, instead of taking desperate steps.

Ironically, when an opportunity arose to become the first employee for a tiny startup, I felt it was way out of my league. I was aiming my job search so that my next position would *prepare* me for being the first employee. Luckily, a friend was there to open my eyes and tell me, "Dalya, this is something typical for women to say. The only thing that can prepare you for being the first employee, is to become the first employee."

So, I followed my friend's advice, took that job, and I was great at it. I took advantage of the fact that I remained in the same algorithmic domain, which gave me confidence and experience to rely on.

That's how I learned lesson 5: Your career can be an adventure! When making adventurous moves, you can lean on a constant factor that will give you confidence.

After six months, this adventure came to an end, and after two jobs in two years, I was ready to look for more stability. I conducted a rigorous and meticulous job search, especially concerning gender representation. First, I found online sources for hundreds of startups in my region, then I filtered them according to "dry" parameters, such as geography, product, size, and of course, the percentage of women in R&D. Then I contacted women who worked in companies that passed the filter, regardless of whether there was an open position for me, and consulted them directly about their jobs. Only companies who passed that filter got my CV.

Eventually, I found the perfect place, even though there was no open position for me when I first applied. It was a small startup, a new algorithmic domain, and endless room for personal and professional growth. I also had the ideal manager (who also happened to be a woman), with a majority of R&D being women. Indeed, I had a wonderful time there for almost two years.

That's how I learned Lesson 6: Once you know what you are looking for, a proactive and systematic approach can get you there.

What happened, then, you ask? Well, as I initially mentioned, I don't feel comfortable in my comfort zone.

During the peak of the worldwide pandemic, the stars began to align on a dream I was getting ready for: becoming an entrepreneur.

It started with a random chat with a friend that sparked my imagination. It continued with me devouring literature on entrepreneurship and was intensified by me immersing myself in the women's health domain, which is grossly lacking in innovation.

The thought of making feminism my day job, of applying all my technical background for promoting women's health, gave rise to new kinds of excitement. I was finally ready for my next adventure.

And this is where I am today as I write these lines.

If you read this in the future and already know my name as someone who accomplished remarkable things, now you know how it all started. And if you don't know my name yet or never will, well, at least you know I tried as hard as I could and that I am having a great time trying.

That's how I learned Lesson 7: Only do things you are willing to risk failing at.

CHAPTER 6

Toxic Environments

In 2018, my mentee Talia took a job as an architect in a senior position. The project she started was closed, so management placed her as a software engineer. In other words, she was demoted for no reason.

Because she had moved beyond software engineering and hadn't worked closely with code in three years, she missed something and made a mistake in the code, which caused a serious problem in production for the customers. Management told Talia they couldn't trust her, so they demoted her again to a junior software engineer.

Talia had started at this company in a senior position with more than ten years' experience in engineering. Yet from day one, she was treated poorly by her whole team. Her male manager and peers shouted at her. They humiliated her in meetings, pointing out her mistakes in public. Whenever she made suggestions to improve code or processes, they'd reject them. Eventually, they stopped speaking to her altogether, writing notes to her when they wanted her to work on her tasks. Additionally, she was asked to stop mentoring someone she'd worked with on the team because, in their words, she wasn't good enough to take on that role. She was eventually demoted, without a plan in place for her to eventually return to her initial role.

After six months, Talia finally decided to leave that toxic environment. She quickly found a position in an organization that appreciated her talents. Still, when she came to me, Talia was traumatized and needed encouragement. She needed help remembering her value because it had been brought into question so often and so forcefully.

Toxic environments can have a huge impact on your career and your life. This chapter will help you identify toxic work environments and give you options for handling them.

THE DANGERS OF A TOXIC ENVIRONMENT

Toxic environments take on many different forms, but at the root, they are unhealthy places to work. If any of the following is happening in your organization, you're probably dealing with a toxic situation:

- Leaders and peers putting down others to get ahead
- Being humiliated, shamed, or yelled at
- Having someone else take credit for your work
- Having your code fixed without asking you for an explanation
- Being expected to do much more than your job requirement or level
- Being demoted without cause
- Being exposed to sexist or racist comments

- Being subjected to aggressive behavior such as cursing, screaming, or pounding tables to emphasize a point

Toxic work environments aren't uncommon. According to research, around one in five American workers have left their jobs due to a toxic working environment.[20] More research in the United Kingdom showed that 64 percent of employees reported experiencing a negative impact on their mental health due to problematic behavior at work.[21]

If we stay too long in this kind of environment, we can suffer significant trauma that can impact our professional and personal life for months and years to come. We can experience lowered confidence, less courage, and fear about asking for a raise or taking actions that will lead to a promotion. Research into the effects of bullying at work and school shows that in some cases, people can develop PTSD as a consequence of toxic behavior.[22] Women who come out of these workplaces are often afraid to speak up in meetings, afraid of their managers, afraid to find a new job. Even if a potential employer has a positive, supportive culture, women might be afraid to take the position because they worry the environment will change and become toxic like their previous place. If they do take a new position, they might be too afraid to act as their old self because of the way they were treated before.

---

20   Valerie Bolden-Barrett, "Toxic cultures have cost US businesses $223B in the past five years," *HRDive*, September 30, 2019, https://www.hrdive.com/news/toxic-cultures-have-cost-us-businesses-223b-in-the-past-five-years/563905.

21   "Protecting your people," Culture Shift, October 2021, https://fs.hubspotusercontentoo.net/hubfs/2138509/Protecting%20your%20people%20-%20a%20research%20report%20by%20Culture%20Shift.pdf.

22   Morten Birkeland Nielsen, et. al., "Post-traumatic stress disorder as a consequence of bullying at work and at school. A literature review and meta-analysis," *ScienceDirect*, 2015, https://www.sciencedirect.com/science/article/pii/S1359178915000026.

The end result is that women don't advance as far as they could because they are afraid to take chances.

WHAT CAN YOU DO?

So, what can you do if you find yourself in a toxic workplace?

First, ask yourself if the behaviors are companywide or limited to a specific person. If you're dealing with one individual, talk to them directly about what's happening. Draw a clear line so they know their behavior is unacceptable. For example, if someone yells at you or makes an inappropriate comment, you could say calmly, "Don't talk to me like that." Maintaining a professional demeanor is key here. If someone shames you publicly, ask that they give you feedback privately and then teach you how to perform the task correctly. It's possible that the individual doesn't realize they are acting or speaking inappropriately, and a conversation could result in them improving their behavior. In all cases, it's smart to document what was said or done and how you handled the situation.

In some situations, however, the person may not change their behavior even if you communicate your message clearly. If that's the case, they will likely not respond to a request to stop, so you should approach a manager or HR. If that works, great. If it doesn't, the next step would be to move to another team in the company so that you don't have to interact with this individual.

When you complain to your manager or HR, notice if your complaint is being taken seriously. Many women find it is not. In fact, we are told they are being too sensitive—that is actually our fault because we can't handle the way we're being spoken to. This response is not acceptable, and you should say that. Sensitivity is not relevant to the conversation; the problem is the behavior of the person who shamed you or made a sexist remark. That behavior is unacceptable.

If talking to your manager and HR doesn't work, your last resort is to leave. I urge you: don't accept toxic environments as the norm. If these steps don't work, remove yourself from that workplace. As mentioned earlier, tolerating it for too long can be very damaging.

As women, we tend to take a lot on ourselves. We feel guilty and responsible for what we did or didn't do. Don't do that with a toxic workplace. Shake off all responsibility for those damaging words and actions. It's not you. It's not your fault. Focus on going somewhere else, somewhere with a positive culture, where they appreciate your value.

DON'T BE AFRAID TO LEAVE

If you've talked to the individual and/or management and nothing changes, *leave*. It's really as simple as that. Your personal and professional lives can suffer greatly if you stay.

Sometimes, leaving the workplace isn't about escaping a toxic work environment. It's about doing what's best for your career. Our next chapter will address why you might want to look for another job and how to go about it.

CULTURE CHECK

It's hard to know exactly how toxic a workplace is until you're in it, but you can take some preemptive steps. For example, you can do an informal "culture check" on a company by considering the following when you're applying for a new position:

1. Look for people you know in the organization, directly or indirectly, and ask them how they feel about the company. You can find these individuals through LinkedIn or by going through a friend who knows them.
2. Ask your interviewer what they think about the workplace environment. You might not get the whole picture, but it's a start. Someone might tell you something that they think is great, but you don't. For example, they might say it's a very friendly place and people go out together twice a week after work, but you prefer to go home and spend time with your friends and family and don't want to feel pressured to go out with your colleagues.
3. Notice what time they schedule your interview, and pay attention to how many people are still at work. For example, if you interview at 7:00 or 8:00 p.m. and the building is full, then you will be expected to work those hours. Whether or not those hours suit you is up to you.
4. Are the interviews pleasant? Are you being treated fairly as a candidate? Are the take-home exercises reasonably sized? Or are they already expecting you to put in a lot of extra work early on? The interview process itself can tell you that the company has a competitive, demanding culture with excessively high expectations. Make sure that's what you want.
5. Observe how the interviewer speaks to you. Are you told honest feedback or is everything positive and overly enthusiastic?
6. See if the interview starts on time and if they communicate clearly throughout the interview process. Do they tell you what to expect next? It's good to know how many phases of the interview will happen, as well as how long each will take. Do they update you along the way? When a workplace keeps you informed and updated in a timely manner, that shows a sign of respect for you. It's a good indicator that they're pleasant to work with, especially because you aren't even their employee yet. It might not be toxic for a company to be delayed with reaching out, but it can signal some disorganization or disrespect.
7. Later on in the process, you can ask to talk to someone in the company who is at your level. See what their daily work looks like, and ask them questions about what it's like to work there. Ask if you can join the development team for coffee in the morning. If you don't like the vibe when

you're visiting, chances are you won't like it when you work there. Another option is to ask to talk to peers in other departments, beyond the development team and your direct manager (a product manager, a designer, a technical lead). Observe how your interviewer responds. Companies that have nothing to hide will normally be positive about such an initiative, as it demonstrates that the candidate is self-confident and serious about the entire process.

8. Ask about after-work activities like happy hour and trips. Are they optional or is attendance expected? If you are young and single you might like the chance to travel and socialize. If you're a mom, though, you might not want to go to happy hour at 9:00 p.m. on a Friday night. It depends on you and your lifestyle.
9. Take note of the number of women who work there. In many engineering groups, there is just one woman on the team. Ask yourself if you want to be the first woman.
10. Ask questions about work expectations. How can I succeed at the company? What conflicts are common here? Do you work on weekends, or do you detach completely?
11. Look for websites like Glassdoor to see what employees and other candidates have to say about the place. Word of caution here: take these comments with a grain of salt because sometimes employees leave under bad circumstances and leave bad reviews as a way to get revenge.
12. How clean are the toilets? This isn't directly linked to toxic environments; it's just disgusting.

By Looking at the culture early on, you can hopefully avoid entering into a toxic work environment.

CHAPTER 7

Leaving the Workplace

In one of my previous jobs, one of the first questions my new manager, Adam, asked me was, "How do you respond when someone yells at you?"

"I yell back," I said, "but I don't like to do that and I don't like being yelled at."

A few weeks later, Adam yelled at all of my employees in a meeting, and then to me privately, he called them stupid.

"Please don't call people stupid in front of me," I said, and for a short time, he didn't, but his overall behavior didn't improve. Adam continued to yell at my direct reports, who started resigning because of him. As a result, I was doing the work of three people because all of the team leads reporting to me had left.

One day, Adam called me about a mistake that my team lead had made and called him stupid in front of me—despite my request.

Later that day, we were in a large meeting.

"Did you complete researching Neo4j?" Adam asked me in front of the group. (For context, Neo4j was a graph data platform we were considering implementing in our team.)

"I didn't get to it yet," I replied. "I will do it next."

"Oh, I didn't get to it…It's not important," Adam replied in a high-pitched voice, mocking me and making faces. He looked so ridiculous that I didn't even get offended. Plus, I was sick of working overtime because his behavior had driven away excellent employees. I was done.

At the end of the meeting, I asked to stay and talk with him. I told Adam I was leaving the company.

"Is there anything I can do to change your mind?" he asked.

"I already told you what to do, and you are not capable of it. I asked you not to call my people stupid and you called them stupid *today*," I replied.

"Yeah," he said while scratching his beard, "people don't change."

"It's not me, it's you. I'm leaving because of you. But because it's sudden I will stay to help you interview my replacement."

I didn't offer to help because I thought Adam would be a reference. With him, there were no bridges to burn; I wouldn't want to be associated with him in any way moving forward. Still, I cared about other people in that company. I had a community that I wanted to support, so I stayed longer for my conscience's sake. I wanted to be a good person and do the right thing. Plus, it allowed me to search without any pressure, and I was hoping the CEO would also appreciate me staying and helping.

Leaving your workplace, whether it's a toxic situation like this or because you found an opportunity for advancement, does not mean you are abandoning your responsibility. It means you're taking care of yourself and your career by moving forward. In this chapter we'll discuss reasons to leave, how to approach it, and how to find your next job.

WHY SHOULD YOU LEAVE?

Leaving a job can be hard for anyone, women in particular. We tend to be loyal. We like the security of a known position and company, and we don't want to open ourselves up for the rejection that often comes with job hunting. We also don't want to disappoint our manager by leaving or make life difficult for them because we have special knowledge within the company. Sometimes we have personal financial uncertainty.

There are times, however, when leaving is the best thing for you and your career. Moving between jobs and companies is one sure way to climb the ladder, both in terms of salary and title. Switching organizations is an opportunity to learn different skills, work with different people, and grow personally as well as professionally.

So, how do you know when it is time to leave? A toxic work environment is one obvious reason, but there are others:

- *You are too comfortable.* You know everything there is to know about the system and the features.
- *You aren't learning enough.* This could mean you're stuck with the same technology, nothing new happens, you are not challenged, and your knowledge doesn't grow.
- *You don't like the culture or the people.* This is distinct from a toxic environment. Maybe the technology is outdated and you don't want to stagnate alongside it. On the other end of the spectrum, perhaps the culture is too aggressive or fast-paced. Whatever it is, the company doesn't fit with your goals and interests.
- *You are not promoted but you want to be.* Be honest with yourself here—is there a chance to be promoted in this organization? If you don't see anything coming in the next few months, consider leaving.
- *Your salary is too low.* If this is the case, try to raise it first. If that doesn't work, then leave.
- *You were offered a better, more interesting position elsewhere.* Take the opportunity and go for it.

Even if one of these reasons applies, you might feel guilty, hesitant, or fearful about leaving your current job. I encourage you to let go of those feelings. It's important to look after yourself and your career. It's on you to figure out when to take that step. If management doesn't recognize your value, if you aren't being challenged, if you've learned how much the guy next to you is making and management won't give you a raise, it's time to look elsewhere.

Leaving can increase your confidence too. When you leave, you prove to yourself that you're capable of changing positions. When you go through the process and challenges of starting a new job, you'll realize that you're capable of taking on difficult situations.

> **PRO TIP**
>
> Some women use pregnancy as a reason for staying in their current position even if they're not being challenged or not being paid enough. The problem is that they get stuck in a position for years because it sometimes takes a while to conceive.
>
> If you're pregnant and are thinking about switching jobs, I suggest that you start looking now and see how long it takes. Give yourself the chance to see what your options are. If you find an amazing option, you'll figure it out—even while pregnant. Take the chance on yourself and go for it. Plus, you might find your options are wide open. In Israel right now, there's such an intense labor shortage that tech companies are specifically targeting pregnant women, guaranteeing quality maternity leave before they return to work. We'll discuss more about navigating your career and pregnancy in the next chapter.

Beyond that, changing jobs and companies will open your eyes to different workplaces and workplace styles.

LOOKING FOR YOUR NEXT JOB

The next question is, should you look for a new job when you're still working or wait until you've resigned and you're free? There are advantages and disadvantages to each option.

One huge advantage to search while you are still working is that you stay on the payroll. In addition, some people claim that potential employers are more interested if you still have a job, though I don't find this to be true in engineering.

The main reason to resign first is that the interviews for many high-tech positions are really hard and require hours, if not days, of preparation because employers give take-home tests to see if you can design and code successfully. This is true regardless of your position, although the application process involves less homework when you're applying for senior manager positions. If you resign first, you also don't need to take days off and give excuses for the time you miss at work while interviewing. You can do everything out in the open.

One person I interviewed said that he had been interviewing for a new position over a few *months*. Every place took a few days to prepare the exercise that they gave him, and then he wasn't accepted. This situation is especially common for junior engineers, but don't lose hope if you find yourself in a similar spot. You'll grow with each test and prove your competency. Some organizations at least give you feedback for the code, sharing if your answers were correct, if you understood the problem, and if the code worked properly so you can learn. Many places simply email a rejection letter.

When they start searching for a new job, some people worry that it will look bad if their resume shows they've moved around a lot. Right now, the average time for staying at the same workplace in high tech is two years. So, if you're moving every two years, you're normal. If you're switching more often than that, you should have good reasons.

Two places I worked for were bought and closed in less than a year, so on my resume, it looks like I have moved around a lot. When I explain what happened, however, potential employers understand and it doesn't bother them. In both cases, I even put on my LinkedIn that the company was bought and the Israeli office was closed.

It is possible that you will leave one company and accept a position at another, and soon after realize that the new job and/or organization isn't a good fit. At the same time, you might worry that it will look bad if you leave six months after getting hired.

Don't stick around because you don't want to explain what happened in your next interview. I think it's a much bigger mistake to stay. When asked about the job, be honest and say that your expectations didn't match the position and then be able to explain how the fit didn't work. Plus, it's better for the company that you leave fast. It's harder for them if they invest many months in training you and *then* you leave.

I know it's not easy. You will feel uncomfortable about leaving soon after getting hired, but you'll get over it. After time passes and you've added more work experience to your resume, you might want to remove the place where you worked for less than a year. If it seems like those jobs are no longer relevant, taking them off is an option. I've even done this myself.

HOW TO APPROACH LEAVING

No matter the circumstances under which you decide to leave, I suggest that you resign gracefully—even if you're leaving because of a toxic boss or hostile work environment. As pointed out in the opening story, I resigned on good terms because it was the right thing to do, not because my boss deserved it. I did it for me, not him, and so should you.

If you're leaving because of problems in the workplace that you've tried to address, bring that up. You might say something like, "I brought the problem to you. You didn't handle it. I'm going." If this is too bold for you, take a different approach, which might look like saying you have a better opportunity elsewhere or you need a change. Ultimately, the decision is yours.

If you had a positive relationship with your manager, be kind and express what you gained from the experience. For example, you might say, "I really liked working here and I matured a lot personally and professionally, but I want a different challenge." Also, you can try to give more than the required notice and offer to help train your replacement or others in the company who will be taking over your responsibilities. Thoroughly document what you've done so the next person can take over and do an excellent job. In the past, I have supported people long after I left for a different company. Doing so will speak to your character and will help ensure your past managers give you positive referrals in the future.

DO IT

If you want to climb the ladder in high tech, you will most likely be in the position of leaving one company and moving to another. It will be the best thing for you and your career. Although the process can be nerve wracking, you can do it. If you're really struggling in this area, review the chapter on self-confidence and remember the value you have to offer.

Also, remember that the odds are likely in your favor when you start looking for a new job. Many times hiring managers are more optimistic about the potential of outsiders than that of the insiders they are familiar with. This is why moving between companies is one of the best vehicles for achieving promotion. The hiring team is looking for a "fresh saver" from the outside.

Leaving one job and looking for another is difficult at anytime, but especially when you're pregnant. In the next chapter we consider this topic, as well as motherhood in general and its impact on your career.

CHAPTER 8

Motherhood

Early in my career, I joined a group called Workplace Intelligence that I found through Baot. Our group was made up of twelve female managers in engineering.

During one meetup, someone talked about coming back from maternity leave. Before she left, she held a very senior position and managed the largest team within the company. When she returned, however, she lost her team and the specific product she was managing. She was assigned to a much smaller and less important product with only one developer. While she didn't lose her title, it was like she had just received a demotion.

Another woman mentioned that the same thing happened to her. Then someone else said that she came back from maternity leave and was fired. We realized ten out of the twelve of us had either lost our jobs or lost our positions when we came back from maternity leave.

That included me.

The day I left for maternity leave, an American company bought my Israeli startup. I was the VP of R&D at the time, and while I was gone, I learned that the US company was bringing in their own VP. They offered me a different role—something lower—and I said yes so I could stay while searching for a different position. Then they offered me another role, something even less senior, and when I hesitated, they offered me something even lower. Their goal was to discourage me and force me to resign, but I refused to do so. I finally agreed to the backend developer position they offered, knowing I would look for another position when I returned from maternity leave.

During this process, my Israeli CEO tried to have my back. He told the American owners that the engineering group couldn't succeed without me, but they didn't know me and didn't care about the Israeli laws. So, they fired me. They justified it by saying that my position was no longer needed.

If I had been in the office instead of on leave, the US company would have seen my skills and knowledge. They would have seen my value. But because I was at home, it was much easier to fire me.

Each woman in the Workplace Intelligence group had a similar story. In each case, the woman's absence or the fact that she would have a child when she returned figured into the company's decision to fire her, even though it's not legal to do so in Israel. They assumed that she would work less or be less committed after having her child.

There is a lot to consider when you decide to have a child and take maternity leave, both personally and professionally. This chapter will talk about what to expect and how motherhood might impact your career.

PRO TIP

Later on in the book, you'll read Rina Artstain's story of moving up the ladder in high tech. Here is her advice about being a working mom: "Juggling work and kids is never easy...Get help. Outsource cleaning, cooking, daily pickups. Whatever you feel comfortable with and can afford. No one's standing at the end of life handing out medals that say, 'I did it myself.'"[23]

MATERNITY LEAVE

In Israel, maternity leave includes fifteen paid weeks off and another eleven unpaid weeks. In theory, your employer can't fire you during those twenty-six weeks, but as we've seen, it still happens a lot.

If you return to work after six weeks, your partner can take your right for maternity leave for whatever's left from those twenty-six weeks. For two of my three maternity leaves, my husband had an additional twenty weeks of maternity leave, with a mix of paid and unpaid.

In the United States, employers are not required to offer any paid maternity leave. In addition, employers are not prohibited from firing a woman who is on maternity leave. Most high-tech companies will give you a salary for a specific period of time, usually from six months to a year. Many high-tech companies allow women to get back to work with flexibility, for example, with shorter hours or working from home.

In Canada, biological or surrogate mothers receive fifteen weeks of maternity leave, plus thirty-five weeks of parental benefits that can

---

[23] Rina Artstain, "How I Got My Career Back on Track," RinaArts.com, October 13, 2021, https://rinaarts.com/how-i-got-my-career-back-on-track/.

be shared between two parents. In Great Britain, parental leave can be taken up to eleven weeks before the expected childbirth, and mothers receive twenty-six weeks of "Ordinary Maternity Leave," which they can extend for an additional twenty-six weeks of "Additional Maternity Leave."

Sweden is the most generous country in the world for maternity and paternity leave. When a child is born or adopted, Swedish parents are entitled to 480 days of paid parental leave. Each parent receives ninety days that are nontransferable, with a maximum of 240 days each. In the case of a single parent, they receive a full 480 days. Swedish fathers take around 30 percent of all paid parental leave in the country. I encourage you to research your country's laws and regulations about maternity leave.

When it comes to actually giving birth and taking maternity leave, know that the whole experience might be different than what you expect. Some women think they will take a year off and be with the child at home. But when they actually give birth, they freak out after three months and want to get back as soon as possible. I know mothers who were answering emails from the delivery room and came back to work as soon as they were allowed. Other women think they will want to go back to work quickly but realize they really like taking time with their child. It's hard to know how you will respond until it happens.

Maternity leave is also an opportunity. With time off, you can reconsider your career and your priorities. You can look for another job and even interview. Or you can simply enjoy time with your baby. It's really up to you.

When I gave birth to my first child, I left my high-tech job to explore my options. I spent time at home with my daughter, but I also took time for myself. When I returned, I didn't go back to a high-tech position. Instead, I started coaching women. For my second and third children, who were both carried by a surrogate, I took a short leave and my husband took most of the time—mainly because I wanted to get back to work quickly.

The important thing is that you have lots of options.

Understand that if you choose to take time off, there is a trade-off. Women often are less likely to get promotions, raises, or bonuses when they take maternity leave. One study found that having children creates a pay gap of around 20 percent over the course of a woman's career.[24] It sucks, and it's likely not legal, but it's the reality.

When it's time to get back to work, find out if your workplace has helpful ways to transition back. Some companies have rooms for breastfeeding or options for a gradual return to the workplace.

Though my husband took two of the parental leaves, most men in Israel don't: only one out of 140 Israeli fathers, or .7 percent, takes a parental leave. The United States sees similar rates: only 5 percent of new fathers take paternity leave according to Dr. Richard Petts's research.[25]

---

24 Henrik Kleven, Camille Landais, and Jakob DEgholt Sogaard, "Children and Gender Inequality: Evidence from Denmark," working paper 24219, NBER Working Paper Series, January 2018, https://www.henrikkleven.com/uploads/3/7/3/1/37310663/kleven-landais-sogaard_nber-w24219_jan2018.pdf?fbclid=IwAR1FiMUULzm6oNRQ11KjvKlemQoL2_cxP6KJQFY1URlpN5sjVmWh0-qYA4M.

25 "Dr. Petts Publishes on Paternity Leave-Taking," Ball State University, https://www.bsu.edu/academics/collegesanddepartments/sociology/about/news/petts-publishes-on-paternity-leave-taking.

> **SPOUSE CHECK-IN**
>
> Before you have kids—maybe even before you get married—find out if your partner will support your career. Ask how you will determine who stays home if the baby is sick or has a doctor's appointment. Talk about taking parental leave. Discuss how you will divide the work. Make sure that you are with someone who suits your career wants.

Paternity leave should be encouraged more. As discussed in Chapter 1, if you are the only one taking parental leave, then you become the expert of the child. But if you are dividing the work, then you are both experts, so you start the baby's life as equals.

When it comes to starting and expanding your family, know that you have choices.

FERTILITY

If you are struggling with fertility, know my heart is with you. Fertility is hard, expensive, and heartbreaking. For me, it also caused a huge career delay. Everything stopped. Actually, I moved backward: as I said earlier, I moved myself from team lead to developer because I was so exhausted and discouraged.

If you do start fertility treatments, you'll want to consider whether or not to tell your employer. There's not a straightforward answer. A potential pro of telling your employer is getting support at work. You can be open about emotional difficulties during treatment, such as an attempt at becoming pregnant failing. I told my employer, and I received a lot of support and understanding. I didn't need to hide my difficult moods, and people gave me space to feel my emotions.

On the other hand, you could also lose out on a promotion if your employer sees you and your contribution differently after you share. Your employer might not understand what you're going through and just fire you. In Israel, there are laws against firing someone who's in a fertility treatment without an unrelated reason, such as a company closing or poor job performance. The United States does not have any laws to protect women during this time.

If you go through fertility treatment, be prepared for an emotional roller coaster. The monthly protocol involves hormones and shots, which will likely make you tired and possibly depressed. You'll likely gain weight. At times you may wonder why you're doing this. You may want to give up. I went through all of that. Then, at the end of the protocol, you might not even get pregnant or you might conceive and then lose the baby.

During my attempts to have children, I had six miscarriages, two while I was in fertility treatments. As mentioned earlier, it was a painful, draining process. We now have three wonderful children, but it was a very dark period, and it lasted for years.

Fertility treatment can be a lonely and difficult time for whoever goes through it. Some women feel really sad and closed off. They feel it's a private issue that they can't share with anyone besides their spouse. No matter what the experience is like for you, try to find ways to get through this time more easily, whether that means going to therapy, spending time with friends, finding support groups, or taking time to participate in sports or other physical activities.

You can get through it; I did. But just know it won't be easy and the whole process can affect your career.

PRO TIP

These warnings about maternity leave and fertility treatment are not meant to discourage you. You can make it work. You can have children and still advance your career. Here are some tips for doing that while you are on maternity leave:

- Use maternity leave as an opportunity to upgrade your position. Interview inside and/or outside your organization for higher roles.
- If you are interviewing for a new job while on maternity leave, bring a nanny with you to watch your baby.
- Meet other R&D women to network, and bring your baby with you.
- Listen to lectures about whatever interests you—entrepreneurship, new technologies, and so on. Gain new knowledge that you can use when you return to the office.
- *If* you are up for it, join important meetings to show yourself and to communicate that you are interested in what's going on in the organization. Don't feel like you have to do this. I'm not sure that I recommend it, but some of you might feel like this is the right choice for you.
- Forgive yourself if your baby doesn't sleep well and you're so tired that you can't do anything at all. That's okay too!

Once you do return to work, you will likely still be tired. This is normal. When you find that you have more energy or you have some help, use that time to do a little extra, to push yourself and improve.

DECIDE WHAT'S RIGHT FOR YOU

One of my mentees was interviewing for jobs while five months pregnant, though she wasn't yet showing. She made it through all four stages of interviewing at one company and was told she passed. Out of a desire to be open and honest, she informed the company she was pregnant before receiving an offer. Rather than being understanding, they disappeared and never got back to her.

Still, not all experiences navigating pregnancy in the workplace are bad. Another mentee of mine used her maternity leave as an opportunity to consider her next career move, hiring a nanny to help her care for her child while she researched her options. After careful review, she set her sights on getting a product manager position at a prestigious company. After months of rigorous studying and interviews, she received an amazing offer and accepted.

If you're like many women, you may want to have more than one child. This means going through multiple pregnancies and maternity leaves, all of which can have a mental, emotional, and financial cost and leave you feeling tired all of the time. You'll want to do it all, but trying to navigate motherhood can drive you crazy. Your career will probably slow down for a few years, both in terms of climbing the ladder and in terms of salary.

This is all normal, and you can handle it! Don't let motherhood and maternity leave scare you. Just be aware of the trade-offs upfront and take the time to figure out what's best for you, your career, and your family. It's an individual decision.

When you bring children to this world, a new complex experience opens up for you. I want to remind you that you are great just as you are. You might feel "mediocre" for a while. It's OK. You don't have to be a super mom and a super woman. It's your way, your time, your career, and your decision.

Also, remember that the world is broken and unfair. We have to make trade-offs. You can't have it all—motherhood and career advancement—without paying a significant price, so you have to choose what's most important to you. I hope that as we become more senior in our workplaces, we can change this reality for our daughters and for generations to come.

Now that we've discussed the common problems women face at all levels of high tech, we'll look at the different rungs of the ladder in this career path, starting with software engineering.

PART II

SOFTWARE ENGINEERS

CHAPTER 9

Looking for a Job

In 2015, I started the interview process for a startup company. In speaking with the founder, I could tell that he liked me and wanted me on the team. I was definitely interested in the position, so I entered the next phase happy and hopeful.

From the start of that next interview, however, my enthusiasm dropped off. The CTO repeatedly asked detailed questions that weren't relevant to the job I was seeking, and then he became upset when I didn't know the answers. Throughout the whole interview, he came off incredibly negative, and I could see plainly from the look on his face that he wanted me to fail and leave.

By the end of the interview, I knew that I couldn't work with this man. His condescending, unfriendly, aggressive attitude wouldn't mesh with my collaborative work style. On my way out the door, the founder pulled me aside. "How was it?" he asked. I shook my head. "I can't work with someone who interviews people like Amnon just interviewed me," I replied.

I didn't care that it meant losing the position. While I didn't want to be cruel, I also wanted to make sure the founder knew the interview was conducted poorly and unprofessionally. Afterward, I just let it go. This was a poor match and I knew I would find a much better place.

Looking for a new job is like dating: for it to work, you have to like each other. It has to be a good fit on many levels: personality, culture, level of challenge, and coding language. You may not figure out the culture or personality aspect until you're sitting in the interview, but you can still do a lot of preparation up front. This chapter will help you figure out what kind of job and company you're looking for, where and how to find it, and how to handle the interviews.

THE SEARCH IS ON

Interviewing for a software engineering position can be grueling, stressful, and intense. Knowing what to expect will help you prepare. From presenting yourself professionally, to getting ready to answer personal questions, to practicing mock interviews, these tips will give you practical advice to get ready for this difficult process. Some suggestions might not suit you and your situation. Consider each one and decide which ones are right for you.

Start your search when you still like your current workplace. In other words, don't wait until you are desperate to leave. If you're dying to get out of your current job, you'll end up compromising instead of waiting until you find the right fit in a new company.

Ask yourself, "What are the three most important things I want in my new workplace?" These priorities can be anything from having a strong team to using specific technology or programming language to getting along well with your team lead. Whatever *your* requirements might be, they are legitimate, and you should look for them in the job descriptions, interviews, and in any conversations you have with potential team members. Don't be afraid to ask direct questions in your interview. You might even reach out to a current employee on LinkedIn. If these things are important to you, get the answers you need before you sign.

Notify your current employer that you are actively searching. Many people look for work while they are still employed, but they don't often tell their boss up front. Having this conversation can be awkward, and not everyone is comfortable doing it—partly because it can backfire. One of my mentees told her manager that she was job hunting, and afterward was treated poorly—she was taken off strategic projects, became the target of nasty comments, and stopped being invited to important meetings.

That said, I've been up front about my job search, and I really liked the flexibility it gave me to be transparent about why I was missing hours and taking days off. In addition, a good organization will appreciate the extra time to reorganize, regroup, and recruit. This is another way to leave nicely, without burning bridges, because you can help the company look for a replacement and train them. There are definitely pros and cons to telling your current employer, so assess your own work environment before you try this suggestion.

Keep in touch and leave good relationships with old workplaces. As mentioned in Chapter 7, these people will continue to be a part of your network, so you'll want to stay in their good graces when possible, to ensure great recommendations down the line.

Use *all* of your connections to find an "in" with places where you'd like to interview. This means your friends, peers from school, and old work colleagues. Find a way to connect or reconnect in a way that feels natural to you. This could mean inviting them to grab a coffee, writing an email, or simply messaging them through a platform such as LinkedIn to let them know you're searching for opportunities.

Join communities of women in tech and use their resources. As discussed in Chapter 5, these groups provide support, and you will likely find women helping each other find jobs and secure interviews. Additionally, all-women tech groups also post job openings and share leads for jobs. Use these communities to promote yourself and to look for relevant positions.

Search and apply for positions on LinkedIn. Many employers post job openings on LinkedIn, and you can also publish yourself as someone looking for work. Employers and recruiters can access lists of qualified people searching for jobs they're looking to fill. Sometimes recruiters reach out even if you aren't looking for a job. When it's time to search, you can look through those old messages, and if you're interested, ask if there's something relevant to you. It's common for them to still have positions they need to fill.

Apply for positions you want, even if you're not 100 percent qualified for them. As mentioned earlier, women often only apply when they are a 100 percent fit, whereas men apply even if they only have 60 percent of the qualifications—and they often get the job. So, if you want the job, apply for it! You might be surprised by the outcome.

PREPARING TO INTERVIEW

After you identify and apply for the job you want, it's time to prepare for the interview.

Check out *Cracking the Coding Interview* by Gayle Laakmann McDowell. This bible for finding work in software engineering is helpful because it gives example problems and solutions, as well as tips on approaching the technical aspects of the interview. I highly recommend reading it.

Practice software coding questions. A great way to do this is to find websites that give you practice tests. Two I like are Interviewbit.com and Leetcode.com. Both sites ask you to write code based on a prompt, after which they will run the code and show its output. You can compare that output with the desired outcome to see if you wrote the code correctly. These sites even have sample questions that are direct interview questions for large companies, such as Facebook or Amazon.

Practice system design questions. System design is the process of planning the system aspects of a product or a specific feature in a product in terms of modules, architecture, components, and their interfaces. To prepare for this part of the interview, do a Google search for "system design of [company name like Twitter]," and practice identifying the elements that should be included when planning a system: scalability, load balancing, caching, storage, replication, sharding, and availability.

Before each interview, find out who you're interviewing with and what kind of interview it is. Will you be talking to HR? In that case, the questions will probably focus on personal relationships. Will you be talking to the team lead? Then the questions will probably be more technical. Will you be writing code? Are you talking about software architecture? In some cases you might start by having a technical conversation with the team lead, and then she might want to have a more personal interview to make sure she connects with you.

Feel free to ask both of these questions—who you will talk to and what you will talk about. Having this information ahead of time will help you prepare and manage your stress.

Practice both personal and technical interview questions. Most interviews contain some common personal questions, for example, "What are your strengths?" "What is your biggest career success?" Because you're interviewing for a software engineering position, you can also expect certain technical questions, such as, "What architecture work have you done?" and "What project are you working on at the moment?" If you want more sample technical questions, check out *Cracking the Coding Interview*. To seek out more sample personal questions, you can Google "software engineer interview questions."

In addition, practice sharing your career path and what makes you a good employee. Maybe you want to emphasize that you're reliable, independent, or a quick learner. Think of example stories to show those qualities to your interviewer. If you have a community of software engineers, practice with them.

Find out the salary you deserve. We've talked about the importance of this already. You don't want to be the one making 10–30 percent less than the men around you. If you don't want to ask around at your current job or if this is your first software engineering role, research "salary software engineer" online. You can also refer back to Chapter 4 for tips on negotiating salary.

Understand the company you're interviewing for. A quick search of the company's website can tell you a lot. Find out what the product is. Learn about the organization's story. This research will help you know if you want to be part of that company working on that product. It will also enable you to ask relevant background questions, which will make a good impression.

THE INTERVIEW PROCESS

The interview process itself can be stressful and time-consuming, especially the technical section—both the coding and the system design questions. Here are some tips for succeeding no matter what you encounter.

Start by interviewing at places where you don't want to work. This might sound counterintuitive. However, because interviewing for a software engineer position is so hard, starting with places you care less about will help you do better when it really matters.

For example, your goal might be to work for Facebook or Google. By interviewing at other places first, you get real-life, hands-on practice. Take note of where you struggled and then study those topics again, work on coding, practice your personal skills—whatever you felt was off. You'll get better with each interview. After a while, you'll be ready to interview at Facebook.

Use tools to manage stress during your interviews. Before interviews, I listen to a song called "Catch and Release" to put me in a happy, positive frame of mind. I've also heard of colleagues going into the ladies' room to do the power pose: they face themselves in the mirror and stand up straight with their hands on their hips. Research done by Amy Cuddy, a social psychologist at Harvard

Business School, shows that this pose actually triggers a physical response in your body to make you feel more powerful.[26] You can also talk to your interviewer with humor or admit that you're stressed. Find what works for you and do it.

Show your thought process. If you don't know how to approach one of the questions you are asked during an interview, think out loud. Rather than saying, "I don't know the answer," demonstrate that you're starting to think about it. Even if your response isn't elegant or as efficient as you'd like, try to find a way to answer the question poorly rather than giving up entirely. Tell the interviewer you know it's not a great solution; that in itself will show them you're thinking about it. As you raise ideas and show how you're thinking through the question, the interviewer can guide you and provide feedback, and they'll also see how you problem-solve, which is a key skill in software engineering.

Learn from your mistakes. Don't be discouraged if you did poorly during your interview. If you struggled with a technical or logic problem, practice more, as this will help you find the solution next time. If you had a hard time with the personal questions, practice answering them more smoothly, both on your own and with another person.

Instead of beating yourself up, look at this interview as an opportunity to learn. Ask yourself, "What happened? Where did I stumble? What can I do to improve?" Figure out what you could have done better, and then get back to studying. Ask your friends to help you review. It's only one interview; don't let it drag you

---

26 Amy Cuddy, "Your Body Language May Shape Who You Are," TEDGlobal, June 2012, https://www.ted.com/talks/amy_cuddy_your_body_language_may_shape_who_you_are?language=en.

down. Remember: rejection is part of life. It means you failed here, but you are not a failure.

Change your goal. One way to take the pressure off is to focus on doing as many interviews as possible, rather than securing an offer. This way, even if one interview goes poorly, you've still succeeded by doing another interview.

Also, remind yourself that interviewing for software engineer positions is very stressful. You are asked hard questions; you need to think on the spot and write code in front of other people. It's quite likely that you will not get an offer. So, change your goal. Shift your mindset, and see that you succeeded simply because you went to the interview.

Once you've built up your confidence and interview skills, eliminate positions on your list. In other words, get picky. If you realize partway through the process that this job isn't for you—whether because of the company's location, its size, the tech they're using, or some other unappealing factor—call and withdraw your name. Do it politely so you don't burn any bridges, but do it. You'll save everyone time and energy, and most importantly, you'll get yourself closer to the job you really want.

PRO TIP

If the interview itself is not going well, you can always pause and tell the interviewer you're nervous. Maybe ask for a small break and grab some water. As someone who recruits software engineers, I don't think less of someone if they need to regroup and then come back and have a great interview.

TECHNICAL COMPATIBILITY

When you interview for a software engineering role, technical skills and compatibility are critical. To identify whether you're a good fit technically speaking, ask the following questions during your interview. The answers will give you insight into what your day-to-day would look like.

- Do you do code review for every commit to production?
- How is the code review process handled?
- Is it only the team lead who reviews code, or do the team members check each other?
- Who does the architecture for the features? Is it only the team lead? Is it only someone senior? Or does the developer have a chance to suggest an architecture and present it and get feedback?
- Do you expect engineers to be on call a certain number of days each month?

When you're in a more advanced stage of the interview process, sit on the code with someone from the team. I've even had a mentee ask to work on the code with the team for a day before she signed the contract. That way she could see if she liked the position and the atmosphere before signing. This is definitely a less mainstream approach, but if it sounds appealing to you, it doesn't hurt to ask.

BEYOND THE INTERVIEW

Here are a few more considerations to help you land the perfect software engineering job for you.

If company culture is important, reach out to women in the company. Wait until a more advanced stage in the interview process to do this. It can be as simple as sending a message on LinkedIn. Ask questions that are important to you, including the three priorities you identified earlier. It's also worthwhile to ask about company culture as a whole. You can refer to the Culture Check provided in Chapter 6 for possible questions.

Refuse offers nicely. At one point in my career, I found a VP position through friends. I started the interview process, but partway through decided to interview for a position at Facebook in London. I informed the first company that I was pursuing a job with Facebook and emphasized that I liked both them and the product. Shortly after, I started the rigorous interview process for Facebook, which included flying out to London. I eventually realized that I didn't want to move to London, so I reached out to the original company. Because I had declined the initial offer kindly, they gave me the position I had originally interviewed for. It ended up being the best move for me, my family, and my career.

Be patient. The job that you want will arrive.

IT TAKES PRACTICE

Searching for the right job for you takes a lot of work; you have to consider when and where to look, what you want, how to excel at interviews, and more. It's also important to look at the actual tools and programming languages you'll be working with every day.

At the end of the day, looking for a job is a learning process. Practice makes perfect. Finding and interviewing for a job takes work, but you improve with each job search. Be patient. It will happen. Before you know it, you'll be transitioning into your new role as a software engineer.

CHAPTER 10

Transitioning Successfully to Your New Role

People talk about putting your best foot forward at a new job. But what does that really mean?

When I started one new software engineer role, I decided to document everything I learned. I kept a written record of the installations, configurations, and other technical data, I took screenshots of each configuration and parameter, and then I created a Wiki with all of this information. This not only gave me a place to keep what I needed to do my job; it also gave the company a centralized location for keeping written and visual details that other people could use. Though the task didn't take me a lot of extra time, it made a huge impression on my team lead as well as the VP of R&D, which gave me a positive reputation from the start in this new role.

> **PRO TIP**
>
> If you receive an incomplete onboarding document, update it so that the next people will have a more organized experience. Doing so will help all new employees in that area, all while demonstrating to your team that you're a valuable asset.

In this chapter, we'll discuss practical ways to start your job as a software engineer on a high note, as well as tips for succeeding months and years down the road.

SUCCEEDING AS A SOFTWARE ENGINEER

You've perhaps heard the saying that there's no second chance to make a good first impression. This is true when you start any new job, including your first software engineering role, so you want to be your best self from the beginning. The following tips will help. While some are specific to software engineering, others will prove helpful throughout your career.

Own your onboarding plan. Sometimes you'll receive a document to follow or get guidance from a team member on how to start. If you don't, take it upon yourself to find out who you need to talk to and which tools you need to install. Schedule meetings with everyone who will help you onboard—both on the team and outside of it.

Joining a company that doesn't have adequate onboarding is not ideal, but don't take it personally. If the company is a startup, they might still be working on organization. Even if the company is not new, you can still make the most out of this irritating situation. Whether or not the company provides an adequate plan, you should take responsibility for your onboarding and make it as smooth and thorough as possible.

Learn what tools you need. This goes hand in hand with owning your onboarding. Talk to everyone on your team and ask them what you need to learn. Make a full list—what you need to install, what languages and technology you can learn yourself, and what technologies you need to know. Learn which product the company uses for its source code, as well as other codes and pieces of technology that will make up your technology environment.

Know that installing the work environment takes time and effort. Creating an environment that works, with all of the software and tools in place, can take a week or more. It's a huge task at the beginning of a software engineer's job. Don't try to rush it. Take the time to install tools properly, work to understand them deeply, and ask questions or read manuals to clarify any questions you have.

Create guides and documents for tasks you find difficult or unclear. Especially if it takes you time and effort to install an environment or learn some part of the product, create a step-by-step guide and send it to your team. As mentioned earlier, doing so will help not only you, but also future employees.

Use your fresh point of view on the product. Because you're new, you'll have a different perspective than those who have been working with the same product for a long time. Take time to share how you see the product from the customer's perspective—how easy it is to configure, what instructions need to be clarified, and what you struggled with when you tried to accomplish a task in the product. Don't be too critical, but do share what you're seeing related to ease of new client onboarding and the customer interface.

Ask about expectations. Don't be shy about talking to your new manager and senior team members about what is expected of you in your new role, for example,

- Who should I approach with questions about the different features I need to implement?
- What is the goal of this task?
- How long is this task supposed to take?
- Should I ask the team lead questions as they come up, or try to solve problems on my own first?

The question about how much time something should take is especially important. You need to understand how much time you're expected to put into testing the feature, reviewing code, writing the design document, and finalizing documentation of your feature. At the same time, you need to understand your own skills and background knowledge and how long you need to complete testing, reviewing, and designing—especially at the beginning. The expected time for a certain task might be feasible if you already have years of practice in the specific coding language the company uses, but if you don't, you'll have to study the language first, which will require more time.

Every organization has its own way of approaching the trade-off between time and the end result: usually, taking more time means slower development but a better feature. Make sure you understand what your company prioritizes.

Record your progress, achievements, and goals. As soon as you begin your career, schedule a meeting with yourself once a week to reflect on what you have learned and what you want to do and learn next. Write it down, along with your achievements from that week. As your career progresses, your document will reflect everything you've accomplished and learned over the years. Reading over this can give you a confidence boost; it can also prepare you for annual reviews and for an interview when it's time to look for a new job.

While the beginning of your job can be overwhelming, organizing the information you're given, alongside the progress you've made is worth the time. You will have an up-to-date record to reference throughout your career.

Be nice to people. This tip applies whether it's day one in your first software engineering role or five years down the road. People like to talk about themselves and their work; listen to them. Especially when you're new, be interested in others and ask questions. People are more likely to help you if you're friendly. Plus, being nice is just the right thing to do.

Don't be afraid to talk in your new workplace. Even though you're new, you should feel ready to sit at the table. Whether it's in the breakroom or during a meeting, know that your voice is valuable. Be prepared to offer your perspective and ask questions. Take a proactive approach to talking with team leads, managers, and even VPs, on work-related topics as well as personal matters. Maybe you volunteer on the weekends or work on side projects in your free time; sharing these facts can bring you closer to those you work with and build a strong team.

Communicate with your manager. Especially in the beginning, feedback is vital—and it goes both ways. Your manager should be communicating with you, but you should also talk to your manager. Tell her what you're doing and how much time you're putting into each task. When you're new, you're still learning how your team prioritizes different tasks; speaking with your manager will help you gauge what to focus on. Be proactive about asking questions and understanding your role fully. You won't be a bother unless you keep asking the same question over and over again, so it's better to be thorough as you learn your new role.

FIRST IMPRESSIONS

I've worked with enough engineers to know what it takes to make a good impression. Being serious about your work, taking notes, asking good questions, and sharing good feedback—including criticism—all show me that someone is willing to put in the work to be excellent in their role.

Additionally, I'm impressed when an engineer delves deeply into coding, environment, and features. People with initiative schedule meetings themselves and talk with as many people as possible in their first few weeks, they learn quickly, and they are open to a wide range of information and knowledge. They want to understand how the product works, from coding environments, to how the product is used, to who the customers are, to the customers' needs.

All of these actions can help you make a strong first impression, which should be your goal whenever you start a new role.

CHAPTER 11

Relationships with Peers

When I was at the manager stage of my career, I had a peer manager who was incredibly difficult to work with, mainly because he blamed other people for his own mistakes. I noticed a pattern: Tom would plan poorly, which would affect the product rollout timeline, and then he would blame *my* people for the delay.

It got to the point where it was impossible to work with Tom. It didn't matter how thoroughly we discussed the details or any agreements we came to; in the end, he would ignore my input and blame my team. I finally decided to write down everything he said—every complaint, lie, and occurrence of misplaced blame. Once I had enough evidence, I started showing Tom what he agreed to and what actually happened. At the same time, I told my manager what was going on but asked to handle it myself as I was a senior manager at the time. When confronted with the truth, Tom had no choice but to stop blaming my team for his own mistakes. He could see plain as day what he was doing wrong.

In the course of your career as a software engineer, you will likely work with people like Tom. You will also work with kind, supportive individuals who value teamwork and respect others. Relationships with peers are a big part of your day-to-day experience, so it's important to know how to get along with everyone. Sometimes that means standing up for a coworker, sometimes it means asking for help, and sometimes it means setting clear boundaries. In this chapter, we'll discuss all these various aspects of relationships with peers.

WHY BUILD RELATIONSHIPS?

You may think that creating relationships isn't relevant to your job; after all, you're working with software, not teaching a class or counseling patients. However, establishing positive relationships with your peers is as important in engineering as it is in any other career.

Just as negative interactions with peers contributes to a toxic environment, positive interactions contribute to a healthy one. Building strong bonds with your peers can help you create a sense of community and partnership, as well as a sense of belonging for everyone involved. A nice side benefit is that when you get along with your coworkers, you'll have a more positive attitude toward work.

Relationships with peers impact your work experience now, as well as in the future. How others perceive you can influence how your career progresses. If you are known as unpleasant and aggressive, people may be less likely to support your efforts to move up the ladder. However, when people know that you're a hard worker who helps others and takes responsibility for her own actions, they will be more likely to put in a good word for you when they get a chance. You can create opportunities for yourself by being someone who is supportive, hardworking, and honest. Managers will take notice.

Not only that, but it's possible you will one day become your peers' manager, so it's important to foster strong relationships with them now. That way they'll be happy to see you climb the ladder and will be less likely to resist having you be their boss. If you don't put effort into creating solid relationships as peers, they'll likely create problems for you when you manage them. While you can't control how others respond, you can put in the work to create positive relationships.

HOW TO BUILD RELATIONSHIPS

Building relationships takes time, but it's something you can start from day one as a software engineer.

Many of these tips you should do just because they're the right thing, such as celebrating your peers' success and helping them out. Pouring into your work relationships will likely benefit you too. This might sound self-serving because as women, we're always expected to be in service to other people. We're expected to not worry about ourselves. The intention here is to create relationships; having positive outcomes for yourself is an added benefit.

Here are a few ways to form work connections that benefit everyone.

Remember that their success is not your failure. Help your peers out when you can and take time to answer their questions. Give compliments and acknowledge their achievements. Others' success doesn't diminish your own hard work and accomplishments.

Make sure your peers know what you are doing. Prior to an annual review, team leads or managers will often check in with your peers and ask how you are doing. To prepare for this, talk to your peers throughout the year about your current tasks, your successes, your accrued knowledge, and more. Some companies have daily or weekly team meetings where you can share this information. Don't be shy; really share what you are working on. When you grow your skill sets and understand, you can become a focal point of information for others. This is a great position to be in as a software engineer. Sharing your work and knowledge helps others and strengthens your reputation as well.

Ask your close peers to mention your successes in public, and do the same for them. For example, if you created an amazing feature, ask your peers to mention that you made it whenever it comes up in meetings. Their comment can be as simple as, "Yes, you remember that Anat created that. Because she designed the architecture so brilliantly, we'll be able to build on top of it." Asking for this kind of support is especially important if you're shy and have a hard time tooting your own horn.

At the same time, remember to publicly celebrate your peers' wins. This isn't simply a nice thing to do; it's another way to build relationships of mutual respect and support.

Find people who can support you professionally and emotionally. This especially applies for junior software engineers. Tasks can be confusing or difficult, especially when you're new. Maybe you don't have experience performing the specific task, or perhaps the team lead explained it poorly. In either case, having someone who can calm you down, point you to the right places, and explain what you need to do is a huge help. While this support doesn't have to come from someone directly on your team, it can be helpful to ask for help from someone who knows the region of the code you're working on.

Help other people as a senior software engineer. Position yourself as the go-to person for questions. As a senior software engineer, you're expected to teach your skills and help others progress in their features. Helping others can mean going deep into features so you can explain it well when people come to you asking for advice. You can also look at their code—even if you aren't an expert in it—and direct them toward a solution to their problem. Being there for your peers both helps them and builds your own reputation.

HOW TO HANDLE NEGATIVE INTERACTIONS

As illustrated in the opening story, you will probably work with difficult people during your software engineering career. To avoid getting sucked into a toxic situation, there will be times when you have to speak up. This section highlights a few common problems and how you can respond.

Problem: someone keeps taking credit for your work. Some people frame everything as their own accomplishment—even if they had very little to do with it. This happens frequently with large features, where people act as if they completed the whole feature when, in fact, many developers contributed. Notice if you have a peer who tends to act as if your hard work was their own doing. When this happens, speak up. Don't be afraid to advocate for yourself and your hard work in implementing a certain technical aspect in the feature.

Likewise, consider standing up for other developers, especially women. It's not your job to be a saint and defend everyone, so this isn't a requirement, but it is a great way to build relationships and stand against negative actions.

Problem: a peer makes unwanted sexual advances or inappropriate comments. The first step is to tell them to stop. Say something like, "I'm not interested. Please never do that again" or "This is unprofessional. Please avoid such suggestions."

If you are too shy to talk to the person directly, or if you do so and nothing changes, approach your team lead. If that doesn't work, the next step is to go to HR. You can also request switching teams, though that's not always in your best interest. In doing so you're suffering the consequences of someone else's actions and in the process potentially hurting your own career. If all else fails, you can choose to leave the organization. This really is a last resort and you should try all other avenues first.

Years ago, one of my coworkers acted inappropriately with me. He started discussing tantric sex and went into great detail about his time with a female tantric guide. I looked at him and said, "Don't talk to me about that ever again."

When he continued, I simply stopped talking to him. I also approached HR because of how inappropriate it was, and someone in that department talked to him. He eventually was fired for being out of touch with reality and having unrealistic expectations for how to behave in the workplace—like asking for two months' vacation after two weeks of working and then arguing when it was denied.

Problem: a peer behaves rudely or disrespectfully. Rude or disrespectful behavior can include yelling, shaming, and telling sexist jokes. The process for handling these interactions is the same as with sexual advances or comments: start by talking to the person. Tell them to stop, that it's an unpleasant experience. If that doesn't resolve the situation, you can approach your team lead if they seem adept at handling conflict. If that doesn't work, go to HR. You can also try leaving the team. If none of those measures work, it's in your best interest to leave the company.

At my first workplace as a software engineer, I had a much more senior coworker who despised the heat. He cranked the air conditioner down to sixteen degrees Celsius (sixty degrees Fahrenheit). The cold temperature affected my own ability to work. I tried raising the temperature, but he just changed it back. I talked to him about it, but he didn't care. I even brought a coat and socks to work in the middle of the summer, but nothing worked. I was freezing.

Finally, I brought a space heater to set by my legs under my desk. He took one look at it and said, "Either the heater has to go, or I will." He ended up going to the VP of R&D—our direct manager—because he thought he could leverage his seniority over me. She moved me to another room.

After three months, he was fired for other actions. I guess the heater won.

> **PRO TIP**
>
> If you're dealing with a difficult work relationship, look back at Chapter 6 for other strategies for dealing with a toxic environment. You might also look at the suggestions in Chapter 2 for building confidence in order to stand up for yourself.

KNOW YOUR BOUNDARIES

You can be a valuable source of support for your peers, and they can be the same for you—if you all know your boundaries and hold them. When that isn't the case, you should be able to stand on your own.

Another important relationship is the one you have with your manager, which is discussed next.

CHAPTER 12

Relationships with Managers

In the early days of my career, I had a manager named Ben. To put it simply, I didn't like him. I thought I was much smarter than him, and my attitude sometimes came out in the sarcastic comments I made in team meetings.

Around that time, I became very interested in moving up to a team lead position. I went to Ben several times and asked, "If a position opened right now, would I be the leading candidate? Every time I asked, Ben's answer was yes.

When a team lead position finally did open up, I applied, certain that I was a shoe-in due to my strong professional resume and Ben's assurance. But I didn't get the position, and I felt utterly confused as to the reason.

I met with the VP of R&D to discuss why I had been passed up for the promotion. She sat down with me and frankly explained,

"Anat, sitting in front of your manager, thinking he's an idiot, and waiting for everyone to see how great you are is not how to succeed. You need to be able to work *with* your manager."

That conversation was a wake-up call. I was rebellious and young and saw nothing wrong with my attitude. The VP showed me the light: my behavior was childish and was certainly not the way to progress in my career.

My relationship with Ben ruined, I moved to another team with a manager named Ethan. This time, I made an effort to check in regularly. I asked what Ethan needed from me and what his priorities were. I made a point of learning how he viewed success. Rather than acting better than him, I learned to work with him.

It helped that Ethan was extremely easygoing—the opposite of a micromanager. Under his leadership, I was given a lot of freedom. With that freedom came an expectation that I'd deliver excellent work, and Ethan always checked it to make sure I gave him the results he wanted.

My hard work and attention to our relationship paid off. Once I had earned his trust, Ethan gave me a big project, which included leading a small team. It was a huge success, and within a few months, I became a team lead.

To succeed in your software engineering career, you need to learn how to work *with* your manager, even if he or she isn't as easygoing as Ethan. Being childishly petulant or rude will not help your career—no matter what you think of your manager. In this chapter, we'll explore manager expectations, ways to support your manager, and how to show that you're a valuable asset. We'll also discuss different management styles and ways to work with each one.

MEETING MANAGER EXPECTATIONS

As a software engineer, as in any role or career, you have certain responsibilities—tasks that you are expected to perform from day one or that you are expected to learn and master. Start here to build a positive relationship with your manager.

Get to know the architecture of the product. You should understand every software component, how they communicate with each other, which technology they use, which database applies, and what business logic to use.

Understand the features that you are implementing. You should have an in-depth understanding of the product: its surroundings, its environment, and its other features. When you have this comprehensive understanding, you'll realize sooner if there are contradictions or problems in your feature.

Write efficient features with as few bugs as possible. Learn how to test your work to ensure it has as few bugs as possible. Use the "Find All References" command to see who uses the feature, which will help you realize how your changes might affect the code and other engineers' work. You might learn that you are affecting more features than the one you are working on, in which case you need to test other features as well.

Solve problems. Sometimes you start a feature, feel confident about your understanding of it, and then realize there are aspects that contradict each other. When this happens, don't simply go to your team lead and say, "I've got a problem. Explain it to me." Instead, brainstorm solutions. Even if you don't find the answer, your manager will appreciate that you took the initiative to try.

Meet deadlines. Timelines can be very difficult to set and meet in software engineering. The work is complicated, and it's nearly impossible to anticipate how much time each feature will take until the project begins. Even then, people are operating with many unknowns and dependents. There isn't one perfect solution that works every time, but know that you'll grow as you work at it.

One key aspect to keeping timelines is the buffer: if you anticipate a task taking you a certain amount or time, add an extra 10 percent to your estimate. That way, if problems arise, you have time built in, and if you finish early, you can ask for the next task. Clarify with your manager if she wants to do the buffer or if you should do it yourself.

Get along with other developers in the team. Collaborate. Be a good team member. If they ask you for help with their code, bugs, or general brainstorming, help them. Likewise, give them credit if they help you. Don't be the one who makes more work for your manager because you cause problems on the team.

Think for yourself. This especially applies as you work with the various interfaces in the organization. Rather than passively waiting for your team lead to pave the way in certain environments or interfaces, take the initiative to investigate, talk to other teams, and understand the feature. This will save your team lead a lot of time and will show that you are thinking like a senior software engineer.

Ask for feedback and implement it. Ask your manager how they prefer you to deliver work: quick and dirty, or thorough but slow. Understanding this preference will go a long way in meeting expectations and in building and maintaining your relationship with your manager.

Ask your manager what works best for them. Don't guess; ask. For example, "Do you prefer that I explore things on my own first, or raise a flag right away and ask for help?" Once you understand how your manager works, take steps to adapt. For example, you might be used to taking your time and creating thorough features. If your manager wants you to work faster, and therefore produce less-than-perfect features, share with them that it's a new way to work for you and ask for their help shifting your mindset. Willingly and regularly adapting in this way will gain your manager's trust and confidence, which can only help you and your career.

Insist on one-on-ones. Usually your manager will take care of scheduling a weekly meeting for the two of you. If she does, great. Use this opportunity to ask questions, show your work, and get to know her. If your manager doesn't schedule a weekly one-on-one, ask her to do so. It's your best interest to receive regular feedback and understand what's happening with the team and your performance.

DEALING WITH DIFFERENT MANAGER PERSONALITIES

Ichak Adizes, a business consultant and former tenured professor, has developed a commonly used theory about management types. According to Adizes, there are four types of leadership styles: Producer, Administrator, Entrepreneur, and Integrator. Everyone has more than one type within them, but people tend to have a primary and secondary type.

Let's take a look at each style, as well as how to work best with a manager based on their style. Remember that these are suggestions. Within this framework, be yourself. You can decide how much you're willing to adjust your style to complement your manager's type. Changing some of your processes might create a more harmonious working relationship, but you still have to know yourself first and foremost and act accordingly.

PRODUCER: FOCUSED ON RESULTS

Producers are manufacturers; they work toward results. Managers who align with the producer type focus on reaching specific outcomes by establishing and working toward particular goals. Visible results motivate these managers, and they want to achieve success through those results.

You can rely on Producers, for they work hard and for many hours. Additionally, they are straightforward: if they say yes, they mean it—and the same goes for no. Producers are productive, hardworking, and motivated by achievements.

On the other hand, Producers can be impatient. Sometimes, they don't fully understand how to approach a goal because they are so laser-focused on getting there as quickly as possible. They don't always take time to look at the big picture. Because they're less worried about what people think, Producers can be loners who are resistant to feedback. They are prone to take on the most difficult tasks, which isn't always the best management of resources and people.

How to work with a Producer: Go along with your manager's ideas. Follow her directions, and don't complicate her with details—if she doesn't need to know something small, don't waste her time in sharing it. In many ways, the smoothest way to work with a Producer is to be a Producer yourself. You have to decide if you can do that.

ADMINISTRATOR: FOCUSED ON PROCESS

Whereas the Producer is focused on the end result, the Administrator is focused on the path to get there. Administrators exemplify the Type A personality: highly organized, methodical, and efficient. They check and double-check processes to make sure they are proceeding according to plan and anticipate problems before they happen.

Administrators respect laws and regulations, and they expect their direct reports to do the same. They tend to be cautious and conservative in their approach to creating results, often steering away from more experimental approaches. Numbers, statistics, and calculations are their best friends. Administrators can sometimes come across as less personal and caring.

How to work with an Administrator: Working with an Administrator provides some definite advantages. For one, you're in a very clear world; you know exactly what she wants because she spells it out in detail. She's very organized and has well-marked boundaries. Additionally, timelines are laid out, and overall there are no surprises. An Administrator provides a predictable and stable work environment.

One disadvantage is that she struggles with flexibility, which you need in a high-tech environment. You might find yourself frustrated because she'll shy away from taking chances, trying new technologies, and steering away from any form of creativeness, which could create conflict within your relationship.

To work well with an Administrator, find out what she expects and do it. You can have your own style but remember that this person needs order. I personally struggle when I work with this type of manager, though they do balance me out since I am not well organized. Having Administrator types on my team gives me space to decide how much I want to focus on processes and order versus how much I want to focus on developing flexibility and creativity in the team.

Remember to know yourself and understand if you're willing to mesh with an Administrator's style in order to have a pleasant working relationship.

ENTREPRENEUR: FOCUSED ON THE FUTURE

Entrepreneurs don't usually end up in engineering management. They are much more likely to start as a developer and eventually take off with their own idea before they reach that level. That said, many CEOs are Entrepreneurs, so you may end up interacting with this type of leader at some point during your engineering career, especially when you are senior and working more closely with C-level executives.

Entrepreneurs are idea people who often get stuck in the vast numbers of possibilities swirling through their minds. Because they struggle with the practical side of putting these ideas into action, they work best when paired with someone who helps organize their thoughts, like a Producer. Entrepreneurs tend to be charismatic, independent, and innovative risk takers who focus on problems and solutions at the same time. They are always looking toward the future.

Adizes refers to Entrepreneurs as arsonists because they are always destroying half-started ideas for the sake of new ones. As a result, it can be hard to know where you stand with Entrepreneurs. Sometimes, they will have you start working in one direction and then change their mind and have you scrap the entire idea. When you try to ground them in reality around their ideas and changes, Entrepreneurs sometimes react poorly.

How to work with an Entrepreneur: Generally speaking, Producers work well with Entrepreneurs because they can help implement Entrepreneurs' ideas. While Entrepreneurs rarely lose enthusiasm, it's very possible that you'll lose yours because of how quickly they change their mind. This can be quite frustrating, but don't let it discourage you. Get on your manager's good side by showing enthusiasm for her ideas and working toward her goals.

Sometimes you can work *with* the Entrepreneur's racing ideas instead of against them. I once worked for this type, and when he brought up an idea that I didn't think would work practically, I put off starting on it. I told him, "Let me finish this project I'm already working on, and then I'll get to that idea." By the time I had finished the aforementioned project, he had lost interest in the bad idea.

INTEGRATOR: FOCUSED ON RELATIONSHIPS

Integrators' main goal is to unite people. They excel at gathering employees around a common goal, plan, or idea. Additionally, they enjoy collaborating and listening to other peoples' ideas.

Integrators work well in an uncertain environment. Not only do they excel at establishing relationships, but they also help maintain them, going so far as to resolve disputes among employees. Integrators listen to others and they are fair, reasonable, and empathetic.

Because they are so focused on the team and the relationships they are fostering, Integrators sometimes struggle with meeting deadlines. They tend to be people pleasers, which sometimes leads to difficulty making decisions because they want to make everyone happy. In addition, Integrators often struggle with rejection.

How to work with an Integrator: Integrators tend to be easy to work with because they care about your feelings and prioritize your well-being. At the same time, it can be easy to develop their same focus on relationships and lose sight of deadlines and other aspects of your job. To avoid this, make sure you continually progress in your own skills as an engineer, take on complicated tasks, ask senior engineers to mentor you, and don't get lost in the social aspect of work.

KNOW YOURSELF

Most engineering managers are Producers. Those who have effective people-management skills are also Integrators. Administrators do take manager roles in engineering, but I haven't personally worked under one, only parallel.

Early in my career, I was very firmly a Producer—not worried about people at all, only focused on the goal. As I continued in my career and built my skills as a manager, I started to become more of an Integrator. Now I'm closer to a fifty-fifty split. I'm still very delivery-oriented, but I also care about people and especially my employees.

Learning your own management style is beneficial even before you become a manager. It will help you understand how you work best on your own and with others. The following questions will help you identify your management type and your personal preferences:

- Do you like to be independent and work alone? If so, you'll want to avoid an Administrator manager.
- Do you like it when everyone, including your manager, focuses on delivery? If so, try to find a Producer manager to work with.
- Do you like everything really organized and to know exactly where you stand? If so, you will struggle with an Entrepreneur manager, but you'll fit right in with an Administrator.
- Do you like to be seen personally and for your opinion to be taken into account? If so, look to work with an Integrator.
- Are you inspired as someone who is really enthusiastic and who encourages you? Do you like quick changes? If so, look for an Entrepreneur.

If you're interested, you can take an online management style test at https://s.adizes.org/msi/?lang=en to discover your type.

Really take the time to think about yourself. Reflect on how you do things and how you work with others. Taking time to do this before you accept a job can help you ensure you set yourself up for success.

Establishing a solid working relationship with your manager is one way to stand out at work. In the next chapter, we'll look at more ways to demonstrate your value.

CHAPTER 13

How to Stand Out

Picture this: you walk into a meeting and take your seat, ready to hear updates on X and to figure out a solution to Y. Instead, it quickly becomes clear that neither of these items are on the agenda. In fact, there's no agenda. One person asks about implementing a new technology. Then someone else proposes that the team add a new code-testing framework, and your coworkers start arguing about trivial details with the framework without talking about concrete actions to take. Another person starts listing off pros and cons of one framework over another, but again, the conversation doesn't move toward a final decision. You're sitting there, trying not to roll your eyes because it's a complete waste of your time.

Does this sound familiar? We've all attended meetings where nothing is accomplished. The group repeatedly strays from the topic. People seem more focused on hearing themselves speak and feeling smart than actually getting things done. Team members leave without having clear action items or insight into what was decided.

But what if you stepped in and provided some direction to the conversation. When you take the initiative to focus the meeting, suddenly the whole group becomes more productive. You guide people to actually address the problems at hand, as well as the action items everyone should take away when the meeting adjourns.

Focusing the discussion isn't necessary for your job; you aren't neglecting your duties as a software engineer if you choose not to do it. That being said, it's a surefire way to make sure people notice you.

No matter where you are in your engineering career, always be looking for ways to set yourself apart. You'll simultaneously give yourself the edge when a promotion comes. In this chapter, we'll discuss many options, including learning new skills, specializing in new areas, and much more.

DIFFERENTIATE YOURSELF

There are many ways to differentiate yourself from your fellow software engineers. Some of the following tips will probably sound more interesting than others. Because there are so many ways to set yourself apart as an engineer and you have a limited amount of time, start with the ones you're most passionate about and see where they lead.

Speak confidently, even when you feel insecure. Let's say you don't know the answer to a certain question. Rather than invent a solution or give the wrong answer or become defensive and argumentative, you could say something like, "I don't know the answer; let me check and get back to you," or "Let me think about this point." The key is to speak with confidence and then to follow through and find out the answer.

Implement projects that interest you, and contribute to open-source projects on your personal time. When you do this, you'll gain a much broader knowledge around new technologies and solutions, such as a new testing environment, database, or queue. As a result, you'll be able to contribute to more discussions on a variety of topics, from your product's architecture to a specific technology.

Become an expert on the tools your company uses. Thoroughly read documentation on your organization's infrastructure, products, and software language. When you have a deeper understanding of the tools, you can establish more nuanced solutions. This especially comes in handy when you're on a fast timeline. Many engineers can quickly create code when rushing to meet a deadline, but they don't necessarily do so thoughtfully. When you understand your tools and take time to look at forums where developers discuss how to use such tools, you can deep-dive into the problem and discover a precise and effective solution.

Know your software surroundings. Software engineers tend to have a far more focused, tunnel-vision approach to their products and features. They have little to no understanding of their surrounding environments—how customers will use the product, why they need the product's features, how those features will improve customers' lives—and are solely focused on their own work. This kind of tunnel vision can lead to careless mistakes. For example, in a big company, people might implement the same feature in two different parts of the product, which can lead to extra work, wasted time, fixing a bug in only one section of the code, and more. If you are aware of what's going on in other areas of the feature, however, you can catch that repetition beforehand, saving yourself and your team a lot of work, and showing that you have an awareness that many people lack.

Remember that the product managers and product owners who define the features don't know everything, and many are eager to be challenged. They see these fruitful discussions as a vehicle for improving the quality and relevance of their feature definitions. Being someone who is willing to challenge them is a way to stand out.

Read about new technology. Whether it's new testing tools, clean code, or devops tools, learn about the newest technology and how it can work within your organization—and then think about giving a lecture to teach others what you've learned. Later on, it might be useful in a problem you or one of your teammates will face.

Participate in hackathons. Hackathons are events where computer programmers and others in the software development field, like graphic designers and product managers, collaborate intensively on software projects. The goal is to create functioning software by the end of the event.

Hackathons can happen both internally and externally. Companies often host hackathons to solve existing problems with a new, innovative idea. The side benefit is as a participant, you can learn many applicable skills in a short period of time, enabling you to start leading within your team. In addition, you can add your hackathon projects to your resume and your LinkedIn page. Engineers recognize what an honor it is to win a hackathon. Whether internal or external, hackathons are a great way to increase your network.

PRO TIP

If you work in a larger company, you might worry you won't be able to stand out because you're simply another cog in the machine. Remember that even at a bigger company, you still work with a specific group of people in a specific area of the product where you can set yourself apart as you strengthen your knowledge, take the initiative, and succeed. Plus, even if you're writing a small feature, it will still be used by many more people than if you were implementing a feature at a small startup because big companies have many clients. You can differentiate yourself anywhere; you just have to look for the opportunities to do so.

Learn new skills. Hackathons are only one place to learn new skills. In software engineering, there are always new skills to learn, everything from software architecture to recruitment.

When you learn about software architecture, for example, you learn about your company's cloud infrastructure, services, databases, and tools. You'll also learn how each of these technologies communicate with one another. If you demonstrate expertise in these areas, you'll be the one called on to solve more complicated problems. You might also be called into higher-level meetings or be asked to lead teams.

Skills like recruitment are often taken on by a more senior engineer, but you can take the initiative to learn that skill now. During a one-on-one with your team lead, ask to participate in something like recruitment. If she agrees, you'll not only learn a valuable skill, but you'll also work closely with your team lead, who will strengthen that relationship and make your team lead think of you when new opportunities arise.

> **PRO TIP**
>
> Far too often, women take on the role of secretary: taking notes while others do the talking. If you take notes, let it be for the purpose of focusing the meeting, summarizing the key points at the end, and reminding people of their action items. Don't be the silent secretary.

You can also learn how to implement small features. Some examples include:

- Automatically run the tests for every commit.
- Shorten the run time of the CI (continuous integration).
- Write a script that will enable running all the tests on the local developer environment.
- Create shortcuts for common debugging situations of the system.
- Improve documentation of the onboarding plan.
- Write scripts to automate debugging the product at the client's end of the environment.
- Implement Feature Flag to open and close features.
- Implement a code format that runs automatically for each commit.

If you gain these skills, you set yourself apart as a valuable team member in many areas.

Understand where your team runs into annoying problems. Collect feedback, hear what your team complains about, and then fix it. As a software engineer, especially a relatively new one, if you take time to understand and fix problems that haven't been prioritized by the rest of the team, you will stand out.

Ask questions. Be willing to ask questions and dig into what's really going on. Additionally, if you have an issue with how something's being handled, try to approach it collaboratively. Rather than get aggressive, ask why it works one way and not a different way. You want to be a part of the solution, not solely a critic.

Focus the discussion. As mentioned earlier, learning how to focus the discussion is an important skill. Instead of taking a passive seat in an unproductive meeting, learn to direct the discussion back to the topic at hand. Ask people what they want to achieve by the end of the meeting. Take time at the end to summarize what was decided and who's doing what as a result. When you sense the discussion is going off topic, say something like, "What do you think about taking this conversation offline? This isn't the main point of our meeting." Or "Let's set up another meeting to tackle that topic." Questions and suggestions like these are a pleasant way to bring everyone back on task.

In taking this kind of initiative, you set yourself up as the one in charge, even if your title doesn't say that.

MAKE AN IMPRESSION

I once recruited a few seniors who stood out for several reasons. For one, they really understood their tasks and they executed them with excellence. They knew what implementation would work well as the organization scaled and what wouldn't. At the same time, they weren't shy about asking questions if they didn't know something.

They also weren't shy about sharing their perspectives on the current implementations, but they knew how to do so nicely, without being aggressive or combative. That combination of knowledge and work ethic was exactly what I needed from my seniors and made a strong impression from day one.

Ask yourself: where can you stand out in your organization? What skills do you need to learn to do so? Then take steps to add that knowledge to what you have to offer. That's the best way to start climbing the ladder within software engineering.

CHAPTER 14

Climbing the Ladder within Software Engineering

According to an article on Zippia,[27]

- 25.1 percent of all software engineers are women, while 67.0 percent are men (the remaining percentage did not disclose their gender or were nonbinary individuals).
- Women hold less than 20 percent of all leadership positions in technology.
- Of women in leadership, 19 percent hold tech senior VP roles, while 15 percent hold CEO positions.

According to a survey conducted in 2021, women only make up 5.31 percent of software developers worldwide. Computer hard-

---

27 "Software Engineer Demographics and Statistics in the US," *Zippia*, accessed April 25, 2022, https://www.zippia.com/software-engineer-jobs/demographics/.

ware engineers have the worst gender diversity according to the same poll.[28]

As these stats show, not many women enter engineering and even fewer stay on this career path and climb the ladder on the technical side. Women make up 20 percent of engineering graduates, but nearly 40 percent of women with engineering degrees either quit or never enter the profession after graduating.[29]

In this chapter, I want to help you be one of the women who not only stays in engineering, but succeeds in climbing the ladder. We'll discuss the technical positions within software engineering, as well as how to progress within the field. In later chapters we'll discuss careers in management.

RUNGS ON THE TECHNICAL LADDER

There are several levels on the technical side of software engineering, from an entry-level junior software engineer to a principal engineer. The specific title names will vary by company and some may have the same name for a large range of professional skills and experience level; Netflix, for example, only recruits senior software engineers, while smaller companies may limit the available titles to software engineer and senior software engineer. The level at which you enter a company will affect your salary and the amount of influence you have within the organization.

---

[28] "Software developer gender distribution worldwide as of 2021," Statista, https://www.statista.com/statistics/1126823/worldwide-developer-gender/#:~:text=According%20to%20a%20global%20software,reality%20of%20software%20development%20jobs.

[29] Susan S. Silbey, "Why Do So Many Women Who Study Engineering Leave the Field?" Harvard Business Review, August 23, 2016, https://hbr.org/2016/08/why-do-so-many-women-who-study-engineering-leave-the-field#:~:text=Women%20make%20up%2020%25%20of,or%20never%20enter%20the%20profession.

When you're searching for an engineering position, research which specific levels the organization has. Most companies provide this information on their website, or you can use the levels.fyi comparison tool to learn more.

Once you see the bigger picture of the organization's structure, you'll understand where you might fit and what your position would entail. During the interview process, you can find out more by asking your interviewer which category you'd land in—such as Software Engineer Level 3 or 4—and clarify what puts you in one role versus another. Know that in smaller companies, you'll see a simpler structure with fewer layers.

Researching the organization's structure will also help you figure out who carries influence and makes more decisions, even if they aren't managers. For example, a principal engineer isn't a manager, and she might report to a team lead, but she has substantial power overall in the organization.

JUNIOR SOFTWARE ENGINEER

Often, this will be someone's first full-time software engineering position. Junior engineers tend to come straight from college or university. At this level, you aren't expected to take much ownership over the product. You work on assignments from your team lead, which are accompanied by a detailed explanation of what you need to know, where to find that information in the code, and how to implement it. Often, you'll have a buddy—someone from the team who is more advanced than you and can answer questions. Your buddy will guide you and give you a better understanding of your responsibilities as a software engineer.

To move up from junior software engineer, you need time in the company to prove your value, as well as to become more independent. This can take around two years, though it's individual to each company. You can prove you're ready to advance by applying some of the tips provided in Chapter 13: take on new tasks, learn new skills, learn the tools, and so on.

SOFTWARE ENGINEER

As a software engineer, you work independently on tasks, find solutions to problems, implement features, and explain problems and solutions to junior engineers. You might be the "buddy" who directs juniors to the correct place in the code. At this level, you will start working on midsize projects composed of many features, not merely individual features. You won't manage the project, but you will design it and give technical direction on how to implement it.

At this level, you're expected to be competent but not necessarily an expert. Companies know there's a learning curve for new software engineers, and that it's possible you'll mess up. At the same time, however, they want quick learners and creative thinkers.

To get to the next level, you first need to show competence with tools, problem-solving, and technology—such as the specific language and software environment—so make sure you practice. Seek out unfamiliar places in your company's code and get to know them. Become an expert about them. When you need help on implementing a feature, write down what you struggled with so that you can practice and review those areas later and establish more independence. Go to senior software engineers for help; ask them what they think about your solutions, and if they would have approached it any differently.

SENIOR SOFTWARE ENGINEER

Usually, this position requires three or more years in engineering. Depending on the organization, it may take more. Many people don't get here until they've had at least five years in the field.

This position's scope is similar to a software engineer, but expectations are generally higher. You still work on solutions to problems that managers delegate to you, but you are expected to do so with little to no guidance. By this point you need to understand the big picture: where the product is going, how the systems come together within the product, what other teams are doing, and how to work well with them. At this level, scale is an important gauge; you need to be thinking about not just where the product is *now*, but where it's headed.

As a senior software engineer, you're also expected to mentor junior and mid-level engineers. You'll provide technical guidance, helping others complete their tasks in the most efficient way possible.

Getting to a senior software engineer position makes you very successful. You can continue to climb the ladder if that's your goal, but know that many engineers choose to remain at the senior level. If management is not your goal, then senior software engineer is a great place to be.

STAFF ENGINEER

To proceed to staff engineer, you'll need both technical experience and some level of people skills. This isn't a management position, but it does require communication skills, influence, and the ability to act as a resource, as well as the ability to lead and generally support the team. Usually, it takes six or more years of experience before you'll be considered for this job.

Many organizations, especially smaller ones, don't formally designate a staff engineer level. Instead, they assign the responsibilities to the team lead or what some companies call an architect.

In this role, you create contact between higher management and the engineers who are writing the actual code. You might decide to focus on a problem that management doesn't even know exists. This especially relates to scale; you'll identify what parts of the product won't work going forward, and you should know how and when to replace technology.

In this role, you might be managed by a team lead, but you'll often have more seniority in terms of decision-making; in fact, the staff engineer title carries the most seniority on the technical side in many companies. Many engineers never get promoted any higher.

PRINCIPAL ENGINEERS

Like staff engineer, the principal position is rare and may not exist at your organization. In 2021, for example, there were 67,851 principal engineering jobs in the United States, compared to 4.3 million total software engineer positions.[30]

If you decide to pursue the rank of principal engineer, you'll need to strategize how to get there. In addition to excellent technical

---

30 Principal Engineer Demographics and Statistics in the US," Zippia, updated September 9, 2022, https://www.zippia.com/principal-engineer-jobs/demographics/; Kristina Trajkovska, "Software Engineering Statistics: 21 Figures You Should Know About," SeedScientific, July 5, 2022, https://seedscientific.com/software-engineering-statistics/#stat3.

and coding skills, you'll need top-notch people skills. You need a long track record of succeeding in projects, as well as a knack for innovation. It's not enough to use systems, connect them, and write them correctly—you need to be capable of *building* them. While this promotion is not associated with a certain timeline, you'll generally need at least ten years of experience.

Principal engineers look at the company as a whole, focusing on its strategy and future. As a principal engineer, you're not solving current problems; you're looking for future issues and meticulously planning solutions before the problems surface. You understand the business extremely well, as well as the future goals for the organization, so that you can prepare for it. Because you're aware of different problems that have come in the past—both in your own experience and from what you've heard from different companies—you can anticipate issues before they actually arrive. Being able to address these problems beforehand is a crucial component of this job.

TECH LEAD VS. TEAM LEAD

Within most companies, the hierarchy includes the levels of software engineers just explained, followed by a team lead, a manager, and then the VP of R&D. Somewhere within this hierarchy, many companies have a tech lead: the person who is in charge of the technical system, in the same way the team lead is in charge of the people. In terms of seniority, the tech lead is at about the same level as a senior software engineer, though the tech lead is not as hands-on with the code. Like staff engineers and principal engineers, tech leads need people skills as well as technical skills.

HIGH-TECH OPTIONS OUTSIDE OF ENGINEERING

Sometimes, people start working in software engineering and a year or so later decide to explore other options. Realizing that software engineering isn't the right path for you doesn't make you a failure. It just means you discovered engineering isn't for you. Your background will give you a huge advantage in other areas because you already know how software products are built and how engineers work.

Here are some common options outside software engineering that will use your skills and knowledge of how the product works.

Product definition: Product definition often works closely with software engineers and is most similar to engineering itself. They are in charge of building the product and providing users with their desired results. They answer questions like, "What are we building?" "What problem are we solving?" "Who needs it?" "How will they use it?" and "How should we implement it?" From those questions, product definition finds what will create success for the customer. This is a continuous process, and it helps guide the product to improve over time.

Marketing: Marketing is responsible for branding the company and its product. They use strategies and research to develop the company's brand. They're also responsible for content creation, which includes websites, advertisements, books, videos, social media, and more. Additionally, they do the company's PR. Marketing is responsible for lead generation, which they often do through conferences and SEO (search engine optimization). Marketing generates leads, which then goes to sales.

Sales: Sales identifies customers who will benefit from the company's product and shows them how that solution can meet their needs. In sales, you can sell hardware, software, or services. The goal of this job is to promote the company's products and ensure customers get as much value as possible from their purchases.

Customer success: This department focuses on ensuring customer satisfaction with the company's product. People who work in customer success need to know when, why, and how the customer uses the product. They measure usage trends and use customer feedback to recommend improvements. They also try to "land and expand" a customer's usage of the company's products, for example, from one product to three or from one product in one department to one product in every department.

Support: Support provides great customer experience on the technical end of the product. This is separate from IT, which is internal. Support is generally divided into five layers.

- Level 0: Information available to customers from web sources and specific applications, such as manuals, FAQs, Wikis, and video explanations.
- Level 1: Support people who have the lowest understanding of technical issues. Often, this level will collect customer questions and data, answer phone calls, respond to emails and social media messages, and do basic troubleshooting. They can also provide basic information on the product's usage, as well as help with forgotten usernames and passwords.
- Level 2: This level does more in-depth troubleshooting and analysis. They have a deeper understanding of the product and more ways to troubleshoot than Level 1. While they aren't engineers, they are still technical.
- Level 3: Engineers and software architects comprise the third level. Usually they are experts on the product and have access to its code. They can provide solutions for a wide range of technical issues. When a customer query goes to Level 3, they address the root problem in the code, often debugging it and/or adding code.
- Level 4: Level 4 takes a product and customizes it for one customer and their specific situation. For example, some project management tools are extremely open and highly complicated. Level 4 can adjust that product to a specific customer's needs.

Remember: you haven't failed if you take a software engineering job and then realize it isn't for you. Better to be honest with yourself and find out early so you can pursue the career that really interests you.

Tech leads and team leads have about the same responsibility, and depending on the company, the positions might be combined. When the roles are separated, it's so the tech lead can focus on managing the code while the team lead manages the people. Both the tech lead and the team lead report to the level above them, whether that's a manager, director, or the VP of R&D.

As the title suggests, tech leads focus on all the technical aspects of a project. They ensure that the product works, and that it shows the right metrics and alerts. They are responsible for technical excellence and innovation, architecture and system design, technical mentoring, code reviews, and feedback. They also handle system design presentations, technical capacity planning, production issue escalation, system SLAs (service level agreements), and metrics and monitoring. They see if services fail or databases crash. Another vital role as a tech lead is coordinating technical solutions, common infrastructures, and code guidelines with other leads. Often about 30 to 70 percent of her job is hands-on coding, depending on the size of the organization, the amount of bureaucracy within the company, and the numbers of interdepartmental interfaces. In general, smaller organizations are more hands on at the tech-lead level.

Team leads, on the other hand, are much more focused on the people. Their responsibilities include giving objectives to team members, evaluating performance, communicating with teams throughout the organization, and giving feedback to direct reports. Her hands-on coding ranges from 0 to 30 percent. She participates in technical decisions mainly because she oversees timelines and decides on priorities.

Team leads also build team camaraderie, create activities, promote company culture, manage team productivity, align with development managers, and check in with team members. They are responsible for the team's productiveness and happiness, providing ongoing guidance and support so they succeed within the company. Team leads often help engineers pursue promotions by giving them the right tasks and exposure within the organization.

WHAT COMES NEXT?

No matter where you are in your software engineering career, start thinking about what's next. If you're a junior, do you see yourself moving on to senior someday? Do you like the technical aspects so much that you want to aim for technical lead more than team lead? No path is better than another. It's up to you. What do you want out of your career?

If you see yourself becoming a team lead some day, the next chapter can show you how to start preparing for that promotion.

IN HER WORDS: RINA ARTSTAIN[31]

After finishing school, my husband and I decided to move to a better location with more employment options, so I looked for a new job. I was young, with no real constraints and excellent credentials and within a month I had three offers. I took the highest offer and stayed there for six years.

While I was there, I had two children and reduced my hours to make life easier. When I was ready to leave I was set on getting a job in a convenient location and if possible, part time. That seriously limited my options. I ended up working 80 percent in a small, local-market company about five minutes from home and stayed there for six years.

These are the simple facts. It doesn't sound so bad—right? I was working, I was happy, I was being a "good mother," what's the problem?

Let's start by looking at that second job right after university—it wasn't bad, but I hadn't made the choice to work there by considering how it would help my career. I didn't

---

[31] This is an edited version of Rina's post, which was originally published on her blog as "How I Got My Career Back on Track," October 13, 2021, https://rinaarts.com/how-i-got-my-career-back-on-track/.

really think of much of anything before looking for a job. I just sent my CV out using a placement service and took whatever they offered. The money was OK. The people were nice and professional. I learned a lot there. But I wasn't progressing anywhere.

Now I had two problems.

The first problem was that I did have other priorities besides work. I had two kids and…I was doing crafts. This was a bit more than just a hobby. I had a blog and, in a way, I'd subconsciously bought in to the idea that tech wasn't for women in general and for mothers in particular. Men plan for getting "old" in the tech industry by investing in real state. I was planning to transition into the crafts space—do workshops and sell crochet instructions online. OMG. WHAT WAS I THINKING?

The second problem was that I knew I didn't want to be a manager. When one of the team leads left (or was promoted? I don't remember), they asked me if I wanted to be a manager and I said no. I wanted to be a software architect (this was before IC [individual contributor] professional paths were common, senior IC wasn't really a "thing"). When they did find a manager for my team, we discussed what I wanted to do and I remember they asked me why I wanted to be an architect; I was obviously not "passionate" about technology. I don't know if they decided that path wasn't right for me or they just didn't really care—but the facts were that they did not invite me to the right meetings (even though I told every relevant person they should invite me).

I'm a pretty confident person, sometimes stupidly confident (as you'll see later), but this conversation about passion for technology really hit me. It is very true I don't have a passion for "technology." I couldn't care less about the latest feature in .NET core or Java whatever version they're up to now, and I'm bored to death by articles about the latest trendy framework. I will study a technology when I need it, but I'm not passionate about it.

Some exceptions apply: pattern matching in python is pretty cool or way back when they introduced null propagation in C#.

I am, however, passionate about creating good software designs and practices that will be flexible and understandable for future generations. Since then I've discovered things like Domain Driven Design (I feel it was written for me ♥) and other more abstract and non-technology-specific software design principles beyond the design patterns I learned about in university. It's a thing.

I don't think they were gatekeeping—they probably thought they were being honest with me for my own good. But I was right and they were wrong, and it set me back because I didn't believe I could advance in the IC path without getting excited about... things I wasn't excited about. I gave up, and again—it wasn't a conscious decision; it just happened.

THANK YOU, NEXT

The next job I took was based on convenience—I wanted a place that would be relatively close to home and would enable me to pick up my kids. You have to remember this was quite a while ago, and not many employers were open to the idea of flexible hours. I remember speaking with a recruiter from Microsoft (!) and telling them I would have to leave at 4:00 p.m. to pick up my kids, and they wouldn't even consider it. Today it would be a nonissue (at a place like that); you wouldn't even have to ask.

I remember another employer telling me it would be fine for me to leave at 4:00 p.m., but my salary expectations were a bit high (they were not; I was deliberately setting them low because I wanted flexibility). Also I was expected to stay after 4:00 p.m. if there was work to be done. Umm, what? They were surprised when I declined to continue the process. Fun times.

Finally, I found the perfect situation. They were looking for a .NET expert, I was looking for a convenient place to work, the stars aligned in the sky and everything was great. I worked directly with the CEOs to define the product and implemented complex data migrations and delicate business logic. After four years there, the business was sold to a European media giant—I had a hand in that.

If this had been a startup, my title would have been CTO and I would have made a lot of money off of the sale. As it was, I got a nice bonus equal to what I would probably get every year at a big tech company and some appreciation. I don't blame anyone; it wasn't a startup and it is what it is. I (thought I) knew what I'd signed up for.

WINDS OF CHANGE

While I worked for that company, I had a third kid and took a nine-month maternity leave. During that time two important things happened:

The first was trying to create a startup. I hadn't really given up on the crafts stuff, but I had realized it was stupid to take all my education and experience and switch to doing something that wouldn't be very profitable. However, I did have an idea for an app in the crafts space that would be really cool and I thought might have a good market.

In between feeding all these kids, I found time to write a business plan and realized that I could do this thing, but it wasn't a high-growth startup, it was a nice business. I would end up working really hard and earning as much as I would earn at a FAANG (Facebook, Amazon, Apple, Netflix, Google) company without working so hard and with less chance of absolute failure. I gave up on that.

Which led me to the second thing: I was doing my taxes and realized I wasn't making enough money. I know, money doesn't define your worth as a person—but it does indicate your worth in the job market. I was clearly being underpaid. The comment all my teachers added to my report cards had become true: I was wasting my potential.

Nine months at home is a long time. I had a lot of time to think about what I wanted from life, and I knew it wasn't feeding kids and driving them places. I mean, I would do that too, but I didn't want it to be the most important and deciding factor in my life. I changed my mind. I didn't want a job. I wanted a career.

INTO THE LION'S DEN

We have a saying in Hebrew: "It's better to be lions' tail than the foxes' head" and that's what I felt—I'd been the foxes' head for too long and it was time to go somewhere I could learn from other people who were smarter and more experienced than me and maybe...pay me what I thought I was worth.

STUPIDLY CONFIDENT

I decided to go for a job in a FAANG company (or, actually, FAMGA [Facebook, Apple, Microsoft, Google, and Amazon] as we don't have a Netflix branch in these parts. I was told to try interviewing for other companies first, but I did the whole "cracking the coding interview" thing and thought I was well prepared. Ah, if I knew then what I know now.

I failed miserably.

My first mistake was starting at Google. My very first coding interview was at Google. WHAT WAS I THINKING? I didn't even pass the screening interview. It was sad, really.

The second place I went was Facebook. The first screen I was so stressed the interviewer didn't get a good signal, so I was offered a second screen. I passed the second one, but not the rest. They were looking for frontend engineers and instead of insisting on going through the full-stack process (which I might have had a chance of passing) I agreed to do the frontend interview loop. My JavaScript skills were not good enough. I did not fail so miserably there, but failed nonetheless.

Then there was Microsoft. I won't go into the details of what happened there, but let's just say I tried for two groups and was not accepted for any of them. By that time I was pretty well prepared, but I was so stressed I kept making stupid mistakes in areas I knew well.

I'd submitted my CV to Google, Facebook, and Microsoft through people I knew, but since none of that worked out I started widening my search, and wasn't getting any callbacks. I didn't understand what was going on.

TIERS IN TECH

I'm sure there are parallels in how other tech markets work, but in Israel there are two separate paths for working in tech.

You can work at an international corporation (many of which have branches in Israel, not only in Tel-Aviv) or a startup aiming to conquer a global market. This type of company uses cutting-edge processes and technologies and keeps up to date with the latest trends.

The other option is working at a local company, aimed at the local market. This could be the IT department at banks or companies like the one I was working in. These companies don't usually lead technologically. And even if, by chance, they do apply modern technologies and procedures, no one will believe it or take you seriously.

I had gone from the first tier to the second tier, without realizing at all what that meant. I did excellent work, really. But it didn't matter because I'd done it in a local, no-name company.

Turns out, that was why no one was getting back to me. Lucky for me, the company I worked for had been sold to that European media giant I told you about. Once I'd legitimately changed the name of my employer, I started getting calls. Amazing. But I still really wanted that multinational corporation.

LAST(?) CHANCE

Dropbox having a local branch was not well known at the time, but it was in my search radius so I sent in my CV. Nothing. Then, somehow a connection through a friend's relative surfaced, and they referred my CV. Another chance at a top-tier multinational! By then I was getting better at this type of interview, having made all those mistakes at Google and Facebook. I passed the screening interviews (two of them) and was moved on to the on-site interview. Exciting!

In the meantime, I got a chance to try for a third group at Microsoft. And failed. Again.

By this point my mental state was less than amazing. I'd started out over confident in my abilities, and now I felt I would never get out of the mediocre situation I was in. I felt Dropbox was my last chance at what I really wanted and was totally losing it.

A few months before any of this happened (but after I decided I wanted a career) I joined a group called Baot, Israel's largest community of senior software engineers, data scientists and researchers who are women. This is an amazing group of women I'm proud to be part of. One of their many excellent programs is "Finding Your Next Job," which offers mock interviews, as well as long-term and ad-hoc mentoring.

This is a while ago and I was very stressed at the time so I don't exactly remember who I talked to, but I was matched with the inspirational Hila Noga. I was sure this was it, my last chance, and said so. The gist of what Hila said was: You've got this. And if you don't, there were other options. I'd been so locked in to the multinational corporation idea, that I didn't really understand I could level-up by switching to another first-tier company like a midsized startup, and even if I did end up pursuing FAANG, I would be starting from a better place.

That was what I needed to hear and internalize. This wasn't my last chance. I showed up at Dropbox calm, collected, and ready. And I got the offer.

HOW IT WENT

I'm going to be honest even though this is a bit...uncomfortable for me: I didn't do very well on the Dropbox interviews. I had no idea what I was doing in the system design interview. Add coming from a no-name company into the mix, and that did not inspire a lot of confidence.

I got the offer, but I was down-leveled (not that I knew what levels were at the time). I took the offer anyway. They made that decision based on the information they had, and I needed to get out of the career hole I'd dug myself into—so I guess it was a win-win. Still, I wasn't positioned very well when I started.

Things weren't easy; there were ups and downs. Sometimes I wondered what inspired me to want a "career" in the first place and if maybe that decision was wrong. I cried in the bathroom. It took time to get my bearings in this new environment.

About a year in, suddenly everything seemed to click. Someone came over to where I was sitting (remember before COVID, when we could speak to people in person?) and asked me a question about something not directly related to something I was working on. Incredibly, I knew the answer. Click.

Slowly, I built relationships, figured out how to work in an enormous and complex codebase, how to design stuff big and small and make things happen in a multi-team, multinational setting. I helped improve team processes. I gave valuable code reviews. I wrote blog posts and gave public talks. I worked with amazing people I could learn from and discovered they had things they could learn from me as well.

It's hard to be sure, but I *think* I arrived at Dropbox as a senior software engineer; I just had to prove it. I also think my particular talents and skills were well suited to Dropbox. Eventually I got the promotion to senior software engineer I *totally* deserved. Later I got a tech lead role I really wanted on a project I was very excited about. I'm not saying this to brag, I'm saying this because I'd gone from a head-of-foxes situation to the middle of a lion's den (in a good way) and I was doing *well*. If I could do it, there might be hope for anyone! Take *that*, imposter syndrome!

Even after all that, it was hard to shake the feeling that I'd never catch up. I'm almost forty and there are a lot of younger folks around who were way ahead of me. I didn't let myself ruminate too much, because really—you can't live your life comparing yourself to others; it's not healthy. There will always be people who are better, smarter, with more drive than you. But it still hurt, a little pinch every once in a while.

HOW IT'S GOING

Then my time to leave Dropbox came and I discovered just how much things had changed for me. I knew what I liked doing and what I saw myself doing in the future. I wanted more technological depth, more platform-y and less product-y work and I looked for something in that space.

I'd been a senior SWE and tech lead for a while and all these companies were taking me so seriously! The interviews weren't easy, but I knew my way around them and got several excellent offers. They thought my blog posts and talks were impressive. They were considering me for technical leadership roles as if I was a real senior engineer! Which, I guess, I am.

Compare that to my many sad rejections just four years ago.

My next role as a tech lead and now manager at Google (younger me is very amused at this turn of events) is quite a challenge, but I'm up to it. It doesn't matter that I "wasted" over ten years. I'm here now and I'm ready.

CHAPTER 15

How to Get Promoted to Team Lead

For the first seven years that I was a software engineer, I didn't really think about being a team lead. When I finally decided it was something I wanted, I had a rough road getting there. As mentioned earlier, I wasn't chosen the first time I worked toward that goal, partly because of my attitude.

When I switched teams and started working for my new manager, Ethan, I made it clear from the beginning that I wanted to become a team lead. I also started paying attention to the team leads around me. I noticed how they interacted with their peers, managed direct reports, and delegated tasks. Using those observations, I emulated them as best I could in my current position.

Eventually, Ethan put me in charge of a team of three developers for a project. Even though I was still technically a software engineer, I was fulfilling the same roles that a team lead would. I took full responsibility for the success of our project. I handled timelines and delivered features, in addition to keeping my manager up to date. I made sure that as a small team, we held progress meetings where we discussed what was happening, what was holding us back, and what the issues were.

When we finished the project, I had already shown my capacity to lead a team, which meant I was quickly promoted. Additionally, since I had already been operating as if I were a team lead, the transition into my official role was quite smooth and logical.

Often, getting promoted to team lead within a company doesn't involve an official search; rather, it's something a candidate voices interest in. If you've been working on the tips in Chapter 13, you're probably standing out already. In this chapter, we'll take those suggestions a step further by showing what you can do now to prepare for your first manager role as a team lead.

PREPARING FOR PROMOTION

When you move up the ladder from junior to software engineer to senior software engineer, your job still primarily involves technical skills. When you get promoted to team lead, however, your job changes. While you will probably maintain your technical abilities, your primary focus is now managing your team, not features.

To become a team lead, you have to want it *and* believe that you can do it. Aim high, and think ahead. If you want to be a manager, start to pay attention to how everything at the company fits together. Apply yourself by focusing on the bigger picture. Think beyond your current position. You don't become the VP of R&D by focusing only on your next task, so take the time to operate as if you're gearing up to become one even now.

PRO TIP

Even if you one day plan on stepping back from your engineering career to focus on building your family, don't step back from progressing your career until it's actually time. In her book *Lean In*, Sheryl Sandberg reminds her reader, "Don't leave before you leave." In other words, don't exit the race before you need to. Keep working toward your goals.

There are many ways to show that you are team-lead material, but you don't need to attempt every one of the following tips all at once. If you do, you'll end up working two or three positions rather than one. Instead, start with what suits you and goes well with your workload, and then try something new when you have a chance.

Understand why you want to be a manager and what you bring to the table. I personally want to manage because helping others develop their skills is a passion of mine. What is your reason? What is your unique contribution? What makes you suitable for the job? What are your strengths and weaknesses? What management style fits you? Are you super technical? Are you good at motivating people? Are you good at managing tasks?

While you need abilities in every category, remember that it's easier to show your strengths than fix your weaknesses. For example, I personally excel at pushing people toward a goal, but I'm not that great at organization. I didn't make an impression by becoming a better bureaucrat, but by focusing on delivering. Play to your strengths.

Express your opinion. When you speak up, your team will notice you more. Plus, you'll appear more confident and more suitable to becoming a leader. Especially in meetings, work to make sure your voice is heard. Even if people don't always listen, don't be discouraged; keep expressing your opinions. If you have multiple women in your team, make a point of supporting each other when someone makes a point, as discussed in Chapter 5.

Tell your manager—and even *her* manager—that you would like to be in management. Having experienced players in your corner is crucial. They can help you see what you need to work on to get promoted, whether that's something technical, like having a deeper knowledge of the languages, or personal, like overcoming imposter syndrome. They might also help you out by letting you lead a small, informal team as a software engineer. While you won't technically be the team's manager, you will have the opportunity to lead a group and gain experience.

Talk with experienced people in your area and express interest in what they're working on. Be curious about what they're doing, what they're responsible for, and how they developed themselves professionally in the organization. Learning from others' experiences can help you see the bigger picture of the team and your organization, and how you can fit your career within both.

Ask for feedback. Definitely ask your manager and her manager, as mentioned earlier, but also ask your colleagues, other developers on your team, HR, and Product. Don't worry about asking everyone but instead focus on asking people who can give you the most helpful information—people on your team or who see your work day to day. When you ask other people for feedback, you start to see your blind spots. Again, you want to play to your strengths, but you also want to know your weaknesses so you can work on improving them.

Alongside that, ask for mentorship, whether within the organization or outside of it. Based on that coaching, make a list of skills you need to work on and then start doing it: look at technical forums, practice code, practice architecture, and focus on gaps in your technical knowledge.

Become your own manager. Dig deep into the definition of the product you are working on. Understand its technical design. In addition, take a look at the people your team lead interfaces with: product managers, QA managers, scrum master, and so on. Develop good connections with these individuals and communicate with them as much as you can. This communication should be transparent; don't try to hide it from your manager. Instead, show your willingness to take on these interactions to help move the feature along.

When you apply these steps, you'll start to become increasingly self-sufficient. In a way, you become your own manager, helping close tasks end to end. When you can manage *yourself* end to end, it shows you'll be able to manage other people.

Become an expert. Write a blog or article about your technical area. Give a lecture during your team's regular meetups about a problem you worked on and solved. Read about new technologies and bring some into the organization. When you do this, you'll both learn and be able to add it to your list of accomplishments.

Guide new people entering the company. You can do this even if you're relatively new. Reflect on what you did well in your first few weeks and months—for example, installing an environment. Take that knowledge and share it with the new employee. You don't need to share everything you learned related to onboarding, only the aspects you have a good grasp on. Don't stay a helpless junior; take it upon yourself to start acting like a senior.

Look at the bigger picture. See things from your manager's perspective. Notice how she handles technical and managerial problems, how she explains organizational news, and how she delivers messages to the team. If she fires someone, how does she share that with the team? If a key member of the company is leaving, how does she break that news? How does she handle group and development meetings? If there's a big mess in production, how does she handle the situation, both as it unfolds and after the fact? After a funding campaign, how does she present the results? Is she able to spin it in a positive or motivational light, even if the funding round came up short? Start to think about how you'll present similar information once you're a manager yourself.

One part of the bigger picture is remembering that as a team lead, you are part of management. You represent the company at a higher level, so it's important to appear loyal. Don't become sour and bitter toward the organization. It doesn't look good if you generally have a bad attitude or if you constantly complain about the workplace with parallel team leads, and even worse if you complain with direct reports. (Note that unnecessary whining is distinct from addressing valid complaints with a trusted manager.)

Take on more responsibility. Ask your managers about taking on new tasks, for example, leading a bigger project that involves more teams and a larger scale of features. Make sure to select something with more visibility that will expose you and your talents to more people in the organization. One caution: as mentioned earlier, avoid new responsibilities that resemble secretarial work. These roles will not help your quest to be promoted.

TAKE RESPONSIBILITY

When you decide you want to move up to team lead, be proactive about making it happen. Don't wait for your manager to notice you. Understand how promotions work in your workplace and look for them. Then apply and communicate your interest to your manager.

Even if there are currently no opportunities, take on responsibilities similar to those of a team lead to show that you're capable. Just as I did when I moved to a new team, show that you are ready to be promoted. Even if you aren't able to secure a promotion within your current organization, you can add these skills and accomplishments to your resume. That way, when you look for work, you can show the ways that you've already taken on team lead responsibilities.

If you've expressed your interest in becoming a team lead and nothing has changed and you don't see any new team lead openings for a while, it might be time to start looking outside your company. The next chapter can help you tackle a big step in this process: the interview.

PART III

TEAM LEADS

CHAPTER 16

Interviewing for an External Team Lead Position

When I decided to apply for a team lead position at another company, I felt insecure about interviewing. In particular, I was nervous about passing the technical parts of the interview—even though I had been working as a team lead for the past two to three years. I got wrapped up in the fact that I didn't know the company, its technology, or its coding language. So, rather than taking a chance and only applying for team lead positions, I hedged my bets and applied for both software engineering and team lead roles.

As women, it can be easy for us to settle for simpler, lower positions, but when we play it safe like this, we set low expectations for ourselves. All of the advice I've given throughout this book about being brave and going for it—I didn't follow any of it at this point in my career. I let myself take the easy way out and used my safety net to land a software engineering position. In a way, I gave up on myself. While it didn't harm my career in the long run—I still advanced to team lead from within the organization and then continued to have a successful career. I wish I would have been brave and taken that chance. At every step, it's worthwhile to be brave.

Since then, I have successfully interviewed for a number of jobs. In addition, I now conduct interviews myself. Using my understanding of both sides of the table—looking for a job and looking for an employee—I'll give you insight into what managers look for in a team lead, as well as the types of questions you might be asked.

TELL YOUR STORY CLEARLY AND CONFIDENTLY

Think back to Chapter 15, where I provided several questions to help you think about your unique contribution. This information is just as important, if not more so, when you are interviewing for a team lead position in a different company.

Before the interview, identify three or four qualities that make you an ideal candidate, as well as accompanying stories of success that show you exhibiting those skills. For example, if you possess strong technical skills, you should have a story to demonstrate that to your interviewer. Share a difficult problem you encountered in the past and how you found a solution. Your example might involve solving unexpected problems, such as lacking the resources to complete a project as anticipated. Explain your solution: maybe you found a way for your company to outsource, you changed the priorities while maintaining customer satisfaction, or you found a better way to use the resources at your disposal. Likewise, if you're amazing at delivering projects on time, have an example that backs that up. Other qualities that you could focus on include good planning skills, organizing your team toward a goal, and creating a positive impact for customers.

Your goal isn't to document every aspect of your resume. You don't want to launch into boring, minute details that aren't relevant to the job at hand. Take time to think through how your experience fits with the job description and tell those interesting parts of your story.

On the flip side, don't focus on the questionable parts of your story, such as getting fired. This doesn't mean you should lie. Rather, explain these issues as simply as possible. Share how the company closed a branch, or the project was canceled, or you didn't see eye to eye with your manager. Still, the negative parts of your story shouldn't be the main focus of your discussion. The interviewer wants to know who you are and what positive attributes you bring to the table. In a way, you're marketing yourself and your skills to the interviewer. Make sure that you're sharing the message you want them to know about you.

PRACTICE THE TECHNICAL PART

The technical component of your interview has two aspects, and it's important to prepare for both.

In one part, the interviewer will ask about the technical components of features you've already worked on. When asked about past successful projects, explain the purpose of each feature, its main components, how you delivered it on time, and what contributed to its successful delivery. Make sure you know how to draw every component and recognize why that structure was selected for the project. Even if you only worked on one part of the architecture, you should know how it fits into the product as a whole. You don't need to understand every part in extreme detail, but you should know your part thoroughly and understand the system at large.

Also be prepared to discuss the architecture decisions, the specific database, the specific technology, what didn't work well, and why you used preexisting technologies for some aspects versus implementing new ones for others. Even when your projects weren't 100 percent successful, if you learned an important lesson from them and fixed those mistakes, you should share that story with your interviewer.

The second part of the technical interview involves actual coding and system design questions. This might be a take-home test, or you might have to complete it in front of your interviewer. Either way, it will be very similar to the coding test you took when you interviewed for a software engineering position. In fact, it might be easier this time because the team lead role is less technical and hands on. You can review preparation tips for the coding and system design portion of the technical interview in Chapter 9.

PREPARE FOR THE MANAGEMENT STYLE QUESTIONS

In general, the goal of an interview is to get to know you, understand your management style, and envision your fit for the organization. I ask the following questions at both the team lead and manager level to get this information. You may not hear these exact questions, especially if this is your first team lead position, but you're likely to hear something similar.

Before your interview, think through your answers to the following. Even better, have someone ask you these questions so you can practice giving your answers out loud. For each of the following, I give my perspective as the interviewer to help you understand what the person is seeking to learn by asking that question.

Remember: Your interviewer's goal is to understand you and how you work. They are gathering information more than looking for a certain answer.

- **Tell me about a problem that you had with a software engineer and how you fixed it.**
    - *From the interviewer's perspective:* I'm looking to understand your management style and personality, particularly how you handle challenges.
- **Tell me about a problem you had with a colleague.**
    - *From the interviewer's perspective:* This helps me learn how you manage problems, people, and relationships.
- **Tell me about a situation where you didn't agree with your manager and how you handled it.**
    - *From the interviewer's perspective:* This can help me see if you insist on what you believe in and act stubbornly, or if you're more pliable and open-minded.
- **Have you ever fired someone? If so, how did you handle it?**
    - *From the interviewer's perspective:* Firing someone is very difficult. Your answer shows me your management style in challenging situations, your care for your people, and whether you are willing to settle for a mediocre team.
- **How will you "show up" in this position if you're accepted? How did you enter your last management position? What did you have to deal with?**
    - *From the interviewer's perspective:* I want to understand what actions you are taking from the beginning: how do

you get to know your team, your work, your colleagues? Do you start by installing the software and getting to know the components? The answers show me if your style matches what I need on my team.

- **Did you change an organization's structure? Why?**
  - *From the interviewer's perspective:* This is a question I ask more at the management level, but I take note if you're already thinking about it at the team lead level. If you can tell me *why* something changed—even if you didn't have a say in the decision itself—I can see you're thinking about the bigger picture.
- **Tell me about a situation where you had to compromise technology-wise on something you believed in. For example, maybe you implemented a feature quick and dirty so the customer could get it on time. Why did it happen? How did it happen?**
  - *From the interviewer's perspective:* I want to know that you avoid being a perfectionist and can instead work on a quick solution if need be. I also want to know how you make up for the quick-and-dirty solution—how will you close the newly created gap over time?
- **How do you manage timelines? Which tools do you use? How did you implement Agile? Which tools do you use for Agile?**
  - *From the interviewer's perspective:* I'm less concerned about your knowledge of Agile and more interested in how you implement it. You should know why you do each setup (such as short sprints vs. long sprints or how often you schedule meetings). Demonstrate that you've thought through your reasons.
- **How do you set priorities?**
  - *From the interviewer's perspective:* Here, you can show that you understand what your priorities should be in differ-

ent situations. Sometimes you should be focusing on the customer; other times, the technical debt. I want to see that you consider your options rather than acting blindly. This is a good time to mention if you give input during meetings and help influence priorities.

- **How do you manage the technical debt of the team?**
  - *From the interviewer's perspective:* A more mature answer will reflect the importance of technical debt, as well as how it fits into the bigger picture. Some developers are more focused on creating perfect code, which isn't as important here. Show that you know the relevance of technical debt.
- **What will your manager say about you?**
  - *From the interviewer's perspective:* Here, I want to see honesty and hear details.
- **How is it best to manage you? Can I give you a task and know you'll do it? Will you need closer guidance at the beginning before becoming more independent over time?**
  - *From the interviewer's perspective:* This shows me what your management style is, as well as how independent you are.

As an interviewer, I ask a lot of questions about challenges and difficulties because I want to know truthfully how the person handled them. Sometimes candidates forget to discuss aspects of their style that might cause problems in certain situations, for example, struggling to say no or being a very gentle person.

Remember that the organization needs to fit with you as much as you need to fit with the organization. Answer each question honestly. Be up front about who you are and don't pretend to be someone you aren't. If you do, you may end up at a company that doesn't work well with you. You should be looking to work somewhere that fits you well.

PRACTICE, PRACTICE, PRACTICE

Before your next team lead interview, take time to prepare. Have someone ask you the questions provided in this chapter and practice saying your answers out loud. Practice explaining the technical aspects of past features and practice coding and system design.

In particular, take time to review the insights into what interviewers are likely looking for when they ask certain questions. Remember: they really want to get to know you and how you work to make sure hiring you is the best decision for everyone.

Next, we'll look at the various roles and responsibilities that go with a team lead.

CHAPTER 17

Roles and Responsibilities

I once worked with a team lead named Dana who had top-notch technical skills. In her new team lead role, she successfully led her team in improving infrastructure, replacing tools, and developing CI. Yet, she still received a poor performance review from her manager.

Dana came to me confused, thinking she had been carrying out the responsibilities expected of her as team lead. As we talked, we discovered that Dana had been focusing so much on the technical aspects that she had been ignoring the managerial responsibilities. In doing that, she had been leaving more work for her manager.

As discussed in Chapter 14, there's a difference between a technical lead and a team lead. Yes, technical skills are required for being a team lead, but your primary focus goes beyond coding and developing features. You are now managing a team of people as they work on features. Your job now involves guiding your team, training them, making sure they are closing their tasks successfully—both technically and product-wise, working with QA to ensure proper product testing and more.

That said, I mentored a team lead named Abigail who had strong management skills but wasn't the best software engineer. Like Dana, she received disappointing performance reviews, but for the opposite reason: management's objection was that Abigail wasn't technical enough.

People liked Abigail and she managed her team well, but she struggled with imposter syndrome and insecurity because of the negative feedback about her technical skills. Because her company emphasized technical prowess in all of its team leads, Abigail had to fight to show the value she brought to the table. Over time, her confidence grew and the company started to recognize her strengths. Her team became quite successful, and she was eventually promoted to manager, despite her struggle with technical skills.

Dana and Abigail each struggled with one side of the team lead position. While they both eventually succeeded in their roles, their path might have been easier if they had fully understood all that the team lead role entails, as well as their company's particular emphasis. This chapter will outline the various roles and responsibilities of a team lead so you know what to expect—and what is expected from you—from the start.

UNDERSTANDING THE SCOPE

Generally speaking, a team lead manages a team of software engineers and often reports to a higher manager of some sort, whether that's a manager, a director, or the VP of R&D.

A team lead often focuses on one specific area of the product, such as infrastructure or specific business logic. They are responsible for execution, quality, and speed of features in one specific area of the product, the atmosphere of the team, and the personal development of each individual.

As mentioned, working as a team lead isn't just a promotion—it's a career change. No longer are you focused solely on the technical problems of the software code or on your own individual tasks. Your job is to advance your employees, encouraging them to solve problems and develop technical prowess. As a role model and leader, you manage conflicts, care for your team's well-being, and nurture their growth. Your focus is no longer on you, but on your people. You succeed when they do.

I've met team leads who take difficult features for themselves because they can finish them quickly. When this happens, however, they take away the opportunity for their team members to grow and learn. They forget that it's the team's job to deliver, not theirs alone.

Delegating and allowing others to deliver can be challenging because you have to trust them to get the job done. In the team lead role, your job often involves assisting people while they do the work, rather than doing the work yourself. Because letting go is hard at first, some team leads delegate and then micromanage, checking every detail that the team produces. This isn't a wise use of your time. Instead, limit yourself to browsing specific parts of the code, trusting senior team members to get the job done, and mentoring junior team members more closely. Delegating effectively is all about choosing the right person for the job, explaining in detail what you expect of her, being available for questions, checking her work, and giving feedback. The more experienced the developer is, the less attention you need to give her for the delegation to be successful.

The truth is, with your many team lead responsibilities, you simply don't have enough bandwidth to focus on every single detail in the code. If you're too focused on the code, you might misunderstand priorities, the product, the future, the limits of your technology, or how to replace it. You need the capacity to see the big picture. You're also responsible for managing interfaces, understanding the future of the product, knowing your manager's needs, and mentoring juniors. The sooner you learn to let go, the sooner you'll be able to better perform the key aspects of your job as team lead.

YOUR DIFFERENT "HATS"

On a day-to-day basis, you will wear many hats as a team lead. Some you will take on immediately, and some you will develop over time as you grow and improve your skills.

MENTOR

As a team lead, you're responsible for guiding the team as a whole, as well as each individual on it. They need to be coached in everything from developing their code to working in front of their interfaces (people they interact with, such as product and project manager) to tackling their day-to-day tasks. Mentoring also includes testing your team's work and giving feedback on where to improve.

In fact, providing feedback is one of your most important tasks as a mentor. I find the best way to do this is through a weekly one-on-one with each team member. This tool allows you to hear how each person is doing personally, to support them professionally, and to give specific guidance to help them grow as software engineers.

CHALLENGER

Sometimes the mentor/coach role involves challenging your people to take on tasks outside their comfort zone, whether that's giving a lecture at a group meeting or on a meetup or asking them to work on a very technical feature.

One way to challenge your team is to use a tool called post-mortem. After there's a "death" somewhere along the line—whether the product failed or customers didn't get service or you breached customer privacy—call a meeting to understand what happened. How was it fixed short term? How was it fixed long term (if it has been)? What could have been done to avoid the problem in the first place? How will it be avoided in the future?

Challenging your team is an iterative process—improving the team, the features, and the processes. It will not happen overnight. Also, whenever you push your team members to take on a challenge, make sure you give them adequate time to complete the task.

You should also be challenging them to work on long-term goals, such as leading a feature if an engineer has expressed interest in becoming a team lead.

OBSTACLE REMOVER

Along with mentoring and challenging your people, one of your most important roles is serving those individuals. And one of the primary ways to serve is to remove obstacles that prevent them from doing their job efficiently and accurately. To do this, you need to look ahead and plan, working to anticipate what problems may stall your team.

For example: your team uses a database with a limited amount of storage. It's your responsibility to know when you are close to running out of space and then to fix the problem, preferably by delegating, so the issue doesn't tie up your team or the organization and in turn harm the customers.

Whether it's predicting how the product will change over time or discussing the contents of your team's next sprint beforehand so you all can strategize, removing obstacles requires foresight, an important skill that will serve you in many areas as a team lead.

GOAL SETTER

Part of your job includes setting your team's goals—creating better scale, fewer bugs, quicker features, fewer production issues, and so on. Setting goals like these requires knowing the big picture: where the company is heading, your team's part in that plan, and why you need to focus on specific features. You also connect the team to the bigger picture, explaining the business goals of the company.

Part of goal setting is understanding the strengths and weaknesses of your team so you can assign tasks accordingly, whether that's creating an important feature or pushing them to work in an area they're unfamiliar with but should know.

In addition to setting team goals that ensure the organization's goals are met, you can help individuals set and achieve personal goals. For example, one team member might want to become a senior engineer. To achieve that goal, she needs visibility and proof that she's successful. You can give her some limelight and help her build experience and confidence by making her lead on an important feature or by having her lead a small team.

SCHEDULE PLANNER

Once the goal is set and the project is in motion, you're in charge of keeping your team on track. This includes sharing the plan and deadlines and explaining the number of points needed for a sprint. During the sprint, you, together with the team, should estimate the time points of each feature.

Keeping everyone on track again involves looking to the future. For example, you should know what's slated to come next for the product. You should also know how heavy the features are. The heavier a feature is, the longer, riskier, and more complicated it is. A heavy feature is like a house renovation: you don't know how many problems might pop up until you start.

Planning for the future also involves creating the timeline for feature delivery. While your team might give you input for how long they think certain tasks will take them, it's on you to actually create the overall timeline. It's your responsibility to make sure everything will be ready for production on time.

You also are in charge of building in buffers to make sure you deliver on time. Buffer amounts depend on the risk involved in the feature.

PERFORMANCE TRACKER

Tracking performance may be one of the hardest parts of your job, especially If you have underperforming team members. The quality of someone's performance depends on more than the quality of their code or technical abilities. It also includes attitude and an ability to work effectively with others.

If someone on your team isn't measuring up, it's on you to take action. For example, if an engineer is being rude or disrespectful, start by talking to the person about what you've observed and what you and your organization consider acceptable and unacceptable behavior. Then give him a warning. As discussed earlier, toxic behavior should not be tolerated, and if the person continues to behave in unacceptable ways, he should be let go.

When you notice a team member underperforming technically, speak with your manager—especially if the team member might be fired. The sooner your manager knows about the problem and the possible end result, the better. Then, you and the employee in question should build a plan together that helps her grow. Sit down and together try to determine the root of the problem. For example, maybe she needs more time to complete each feature, and if she's given that, the quality of her work will go up. Maybe she has a knowledge gap that she needs to fill. It could even be that she's under emotional duress at home and is struggling professionally because of it. Together, you should try to analyze the problem so that you can come up with a solution for the employee to improve.

Once on an improvement plan, your employee has the tools and potential to succeed. If she doesn't, however, it's better to fire her. Keeping someone on when they can't perform as needed is a burden to your team. In a way, you're implying that poor performance is acceptable, which can be demoralizing to other team members.

Firing someone is one of the hardest things to do as a manager, but you can't avoid it just because you feel bad for the person. As a lead, you should prioritize the quality of your team. Also remember that it's a good experience for you to have as a manager, as you will run into this dilemma many times in your career. Don't avoid it, since avoiding it leads to a mediocre team.

When it comes to working with difficult people, take note of how your organization handles it. If the company wants to keep a difficult employee because of her technical skills, dig deeper so you can understand the full situation. Does this person truly have an opportunity to improve? Or does the company tend to keep toxic people?

If the person in question is simply strange or introverted, she can still work well with the team. However, if she has exhibited toxic behavior and is unwilling to change after warnings, and if the company is unwilling to let her go despite that behavior, you likely have a toxic work environment on your hands and you might consider leaving yourself.

> ## TIPS FOR FIRING SOMEONE
>
> Start with an improvement plan. This involves a frank discussion where you explain that the person is not performing well enough and then initiate a plan to help improve the situation. Set specific goals that will help the team member achieve success. If he meets those goals, you can eventually transition him out of the improvement plan.
>
> When people are on an improvement plan, they usually know they may be fired. Give them regular feedback during a period of one to two months; this will help them gauge if they're at risk. Sometimes they'll even seek out a job at a different company.
>
> If the improvement plan didn't succeed and the person didn't improve, it's your responsibility to fire him. The process you follow must, of course, align with your country's laws.
>
> When it comes to the actual conversation, state that you had hoped the person would improve, but that hasn't happened. Say that while you're sad, you have no choice but to let him go. Keep it short. The person will probably not be surprised because he's already been on the improvement plan.

ATMOSPHERE SETTER

As the team lead, you set the atmosphere for your team. Your behavior, attitude, and words determine how the team behaves and in turn, how your team feels about the organization. Part of this means not trashing the organization or other employees.

One way to contribute positively to the environment is to have a weekly team meeting. During the meeting, encourage everyone to share what they are working on and how it's going. Then you can share your priorities for the week, as well as challenges, directions, and goals. While this meeting will have a technical component, try to make it friendly and fun so you set a supportive tone for the team.

Building your team's atmosphere doesn't require one specific approach; work with your own personal style. Certain people will want to work with you based on how you lead. For example, my style is friendly management, which draws certain individuals. Other people prefer a colder or more formal atmosphere. Don't try to be someone who you aren't. People want to feel that you are genuine.

NETWORKER

Some projects require two teams or more. Your team might rely on the infrastructure built by another team, or they might build upon a feature created by another team.

Whenever your team needs to network with another, your responsibility is to coordinate the interaction to ensure a smooth process. This means defining boundaries, needs, and timelines, as well as creating positive relationships so the project can succeed. This doesn't mean you do all the communication yourself, but you do need to start it and set the tone.

One way to build good relationships is by establishing clear agreements on how you work together—both technically and personally. On the technical side, this might mean agreeing on timelines, interfaces, and APIs (Application Programming Interfaces). Personally, this might mean having the two teams join together for a fun activity away from work. Your teams are working together toward a common goal, so the collaboration should be approached like a partnership.

As the chief networker, your job also involves working closely with the Product team. They need to understand your team's challenges, problems, technical debt, abilities, and pace. Building this relationship includes understanding Product's own challenges, pace, and timelines. When you communicate these things to the Product team and build that relationship, it will be easier to work together. You can overcome problems and obstacles, while working toward mutual success.

The team lead is the main communication channel between the product manager and the team. High-level feature definition, detailed feature definitions, grooming, and release planning all start with the product manager, who then funnels the information to the team lead, who passes it on to her team. The team lead orchestrates all of these processes, making sure each team member is completing their tasks efficiently and on time.

Whatever you do, don't be the one who creates conflict with other teams. Avoid blaming others, not delivering on your promises, and starting arguments.

MANAGER SUPPORTER

Though one of your biggest responsibilities is mentoring and supporting your team, you also have another person to support: your manager. As a team lead, your manager is your main client or customer, the main person you should impress and please. Your goals, plans, and vision should be compatible with hers, and you should seek to make her happy with the work you're doing.

One great way to succeed is to know how to manage your manager—that is, cultivate a harmonious working relationship in which you work toward mutual goals and mutual understanding. Do what you can to help your manager with her specific concerns and show yourself trustworthy. Not only will you create a positive relationship of mutual trust, but you'll get the added benefit of having extra sway in her decisions.

Ultimately, you need to find a way to make what you both want work *together*.

For example, you might want to focus on creating cleaner code. No one in management will be interested in that. However, if you explain that once you create cleaner code, you can improve the scale of the service you're responsible for and therefore serve more customers faster, management might take interest. Or perhaps you want to change the architecture of the service you implemented. Stating, "We will have better code" won't interest management. However, if you explain that changing the architecture will enable you to build new features much faster, they're more likely to see the value in it. Know how to explain your goals to your manager.

I've worked with women who struggled to align themselves with their manager. For example, Dana from the beginning of the chapter was very focused on improving the technology situation for the team. Meanwhile, her manager focused on delivery, prioritizing the bigger picture and the company's interest.

While she was a good team lead, Dana experienced a lot of conflict with her manager—they each became frustrated with the other. At one point, Dana considered leaving the company.

When I sat down with her, I explained that being a technical person and a nice person wasn't enough. She needed to deliver what her manager asked for. She could do this while maintaining what was important to her: great code and technical issues. Dana's priorities didn't contradict her manager's; she just needed to shift her attention to take them both into account. She also needed to figure out how to communicate with her manager.

Even if you try to be a manager supporter, it may simply be that you and your manager aren't a good fit, and you might need to find another group within the company or go elsewhere.

TWO JOBS IN ONE

In my opinion, working as a team lead is the hardest role in engineering because you have to work both in software engineering and in people management. It's like doing two jobs, and often it requires the most hours.

Once you become a team lead and see what it requires, you might realize it isn't for you. That's not a failure. You can't really know what's involved in a management position until you get there, and many before you have gone back to the software engineer position after seeing what it entails. It is both common and acceptable in the software engineering field.

One of your responsibilities as a team lead is to train new employees. We'll discuss this in the next chapter.

CHAPTER 18

Training New Employees

When I was a team lead, I had a peer named Nathan who didn't take the time to schedule one-on-ones with his direct reports to give them feedback on their performance. At the same time, he would blow up at people when they did something he didn't like. When direct reports were able to get Nathan to meet with them, he was disorganized and gave the impression that questions weren't welcome. As a result, his team felt like they were left to figure things out on their own and then penalized when they didn't get it right.

As you can imagine, his team felt frustrated, as well as lonely and unsupported.

As team lead, it's your responsibility to make sure this doesn't happen. Your team should not have to initiate meetings with you or feel like they are imposing if they ask questions. Training new employees and supporting them as they grow is a big part of your job as team lead. In this chapter, we'll discuss how to carry out this responsibility successfully.

SET NEW TEAM MEMBERS UP FOR SUCCESS

Helping software engineers enter their new position smoothly greatly impacts their feelings toward you and the team. From day one, it's important to make them feel like you were prepared for their arrival, that you had a comprehensive onboarding plan, and that they were given meaningful training to set them up for success.

The following ideas will get you started.

Give new employees time to learn and ask questions. As seen in the opening story, having the freedom to ask questions is very important to employees. It encourages them to think carefully about their job and learn as much as they can, knowing that if they get stuck, they can ask even the most trivial questions.

In addition, provide your team with a list of resources and plenty of time to learn the product, its architecture, the technical challenges facing them, and the team's technical debt. When you give them the time to really study these different aspects of their job, they may surprise you and fix some of the existing problems on their own.

They may also need time to learn common development tools, common frameworks such as CI, the backend framework, monitoring, test-driven design, and clean code. If they don't know the programming language well, you should also give them time to learn that, as well as the technical details of the code and project structure and the trade-offs implemented in the code. For example, to finish quickly, developers may have written the code "quick and dirty," but as a result, it isn't clean or well organized. One trade-off is that the code is functional, but it might be more difficult for new developers to come in and understand it. Another trade-off is that the simple database works well *now* but won't in another few months when the company scales up.

Encourage new employees to speak with every member of the team, so they get to know each person and what part of the feature and/or product they are responsible for. Document both the team lead's conversations with the new employee and the employee's discussions with various team members. These recordings will be helpful in onboarding new employees down the road.

Remind yourself that training is ongoing. Especially when it comes to more complicated tasks, your new employee might ask several follow-up questions. This is to be expected and is not a reflection on her ability to handle the work. Rather than wondering why she keeps asking questions, go in assuming that she'll have questions to ask. While questions shouldn't be endless, they will happen and should be welcomed. Training doesn't stop after the first few weeks. You should be available to give her feedback and help her with design and code reviews.

Give them their first task. For example, you could have someone fix bugs or implement a very simple, uncomplicated feature. I often do this within the first few days, while the employee is still studying materials and learning the basics, though it does depend on the person's experience level. I start with an initial detailed explanation, then ask them how long they think it will take them to complete the task. Once they give me an estimate, I check in during the middle of that time frame.

Talk to them about the culture of the organization, your expectations, and the company's expectations for its employees. This includes expectations around hours, lunches (Does the team eat together? Is lunch taken at a certain time?), and attendance at all-hands meetings or happy hours. Assign them a buddy, someone who can help them both technically and personally: understanding who's who, knowing how to get help, introducing them to the whole team, even giving advice on where to eat or find best coffee spots.

Have one-on-one meetings with each new employee. We've already shown the importance of this action. One-on-ones are the best way to know what someone is working on, as well as what's going on with her both personally and professionally. Use this as an opportunity to get to know her and build a relationship.

As part of these meetings, make sure to find out how she's handling the work in her new position. You don't need to actually sit down and watch her work, but check the results and ask questions during your one-on-ones. Let her talk about her current code, explain why she made the decisions she did, and ask any lingering questions. You can also use this time to discuss future tasks in detail.

Let me emphasize this again: Don't miss out on these one-on-ones. If you don't take the time to check in regularly, your new employee might get confused about your expectations, or feel like you don't care about her or the fact that she's joined the team.

Give actionable, clear feedback. This applies to planned one-on-ones or anytime you observe new employees at work. Good feedback starts with sharing what someone has done well, which will help them tune in and really listen. If they have something to improve upon, be specific about what that improvement looks like. Don't be vague; they need to understand exactly what your expectations are. For example, rather than say something like, "You didn't perform this task well," be more precise: "Your code wasn't clean enough, and didn't follow R&D guidelines. I expected the task to take X amount of time. Let's look together and understand why it took you longer than that."

From there, ask the employee what steps she'll take to improve. Don't let her generalize by saying something like, "I will try to improve." Instead, the steps should be something like, "I will read the clean code document and when I am stuck, I will ask someone from the team sooner and will not dwell on the problem alone for days." Finish by saying something like, "I'm confident we can work it out and succeed together."

Many managers and team leads don't know how to elaborate on their feedback. They might say something vague like, "You're not being technological enough." To the employee, this might mean they're making errors in the code or that they're not able to handle complicated features, but the manager might mean something completely different—for example, that the person is not being assertive enough in meetings. More helpful feedback would be something like, "When you're in a meeting, show more confidence. Say 'I am sure I can learn it' or 'I have a knowledge gap and I will fill it.'"

Make sure your feedback identifies the exact issue and what the employee needs to do to fix it.

SET THE TONE

Know that your new employee's entry into her job is a crucial time to set her up for success. Build a strong relationship with her. Remember that training isn't a one-time thing. You should expect questions and be ready to answer. During these first few weeks and months, you're setting the tone for her entire experience in your organization and under you as a team lead. Make it a positive start.

CHAPTER 19

Grow to Your Next Position

As a team lead at one company, I started with four people on my team. Over time, I grew my team more and more, both through hiring and through people from other teams being added. This happened gradually, as I continued to prove that I could take on responsibility and work successfully. I never refused new people or new projects. During meetings where new features were considered, I would volunteer my team to take it on. Over time, we grew to a large team, and my work started to shift from a team lead's amount of responsibility into that of a manager. By the time I was promoted from team lead to manager, I had twelve people on my team.

The shift from team lead to manager involves doing more of the same: managing more people, more projects, more timelines. If you show that you can handle more while you are still a team lead, you set yourself up for a quicker promotion and a smooth transition into your new role.

This chapter, while short, covers important tips to help you prepare for a promotion to manager by acting like one now.

SHOWING YOU'RE READY

Simply put, preparing for a manager role involves building the skills you already use as a team lead. To get that promotion, you need to show that you can do more.

When you're looking to become a manager, there are certain baseline things you should be doing already—acting professionally, speaking well of your organization and manager, not gossiping about issues, and working independently, to name a few. You will continue acting in these ways, only at a higher level with more responsibilities in terms of projects and people.

In addition, as you progress in management roles, you'll have to lead in more and more areas that aren't part of your expertise. Managing these foreign areas successfully shows that you're prepared for the next step.

Occasionally, I have women approach me for advice about bringing on more people into their group. They worry that they won't be able to handle the pressure of managing more personalities and responsibilities.

Another common concern is that they won't have expertise on all the topics they are asked to manage. The truth is, when you advance in the management hierarchy, you will start managing areas that you don't understand. While it's great to learn as much as you can, often your team members will be the experts on the subject, not you. They will get into the details, while you will stay at a high level. In one of my roles as VP of R&D, part of my job included managing frontend work and data science, but my main experience was in backend, so I had to rely on my team. While managing parts of the system you're unfamiliar with is challenging, it's also part of being a manager. Your role will require some level of uncertainty and vagueness.

As mentioned, the best way to stand out as management material is to grow your responsibilities and your team. Managers have different opinions regarding how many people is the perfect number to manage. I think it's five, because beyond that, it's hard to give the necessary attention to each of your employees.

If your team starts approaching seven or more people, start looking for people who are ready to lead themselves and then coach them into this new role. You don't have to give someone an official promotion for her to take on responsibility over delivery, tasks, or people.

When you do this, it's a win-win. You get to practice managing other managers and all of its unique difficulties. You'll learn how to let go of the details, how to trust someone else, and how to let go when you need to let go. At the same time, your employee will gain valuable skills and a sense of empowerment, even if she isn't promoted at your company.

When you grow your team in this way, you can start to manage a few unofficial leads under you. Relay this information to your own manager; share which areas you're managing, how you're growing your team, and which team members are ready for a promotion once the group is big enough.

In all of these ways, start acting like a manager even if you don't officially hold that title yet, and that promotion will be yours soon enough.

START GROWING

The transition from a team lead to a manager isn't a huge change; it's just about doing more and being able to scale up. Whatever you're doing as a team lead, do more of it. Before you know it, you'll be managing other managers, which is the subject of Part IV.

IN HER WORDS: AYELET BENJAMINI

I started my career in tech in an untraditional way. I was always good with numbers and constantly seeking the underlying reasons that can explain behaviors around us. My friends used to (well, they still do) make fun of me for always trying to find patterns, even in simple matters like, "I wonder why they assigned us these particular seats on the plane." And so, a career as a scientist seemed like the right fit. I did my undergrad in Physics and Chemistry and went on to pursue a PhD in Computational Chemistry. My path was set out for me. There was only one issue—I didn't enjoy it as much as I thought.

Having freedom to research any topic I wanted seemed to come with a price that I didn't realize up front. Lack of direct feedback on the work I was doing made my work as a researcher frustrating and demotivating. Researchers around me were mostly working independently. There was no sense of shared progress or working toward a shared goal, which made it particularly hard for me to celebrate achievements and feel like I was on the right path.

Lesson 1: Your job shouldn't just "sound right" or "tick all the boxes." It should also feel right for you. *HOW the job is done is often more important than WHAT job is done.*

After a long inner struggle (and after finishing my PhD), I chose to leave academia and seek a position in tech, which I'm grateful for in retrospect. Having the "wrong" or at least nonstandard background made the search particularly challenging—mostly because I wasn't confident that my skills and knowledge would be applicable.

I quickly learned that I was wrong to think that.

Within a couple of months, I got a position as a Software Engineer at Google, and shortly after became a Technical Lead, impacting the technical and project direction of a small set of (mostly newly hired) engineers around me. It turned out that being able to question basic assumptions, thinking outside the box, and always trying to understand numbers were all very useful skills in tech.

Two years into being a SWE and a TL, my husband and I decided to relocate to Israel for family reasons. This was a big shift in my career—I was doing well on the team, getting credit from my manager, and getting respect from team members as the technical authority, having built the system that they were contributing to. I was anxious that I wouldn't find such interesting opportunities for myself at the Israeli office.

I set out to meet with a lot of different leads in the Israeli office to understand what my options were, fearing they would be limited. There was one manager in particular whom I was very impressed with, but I wasn't sure how or if they'd be willing to find a spot for me on their org. They described the team where they might have an opening—a well-established, high-performing team—but it was when I asked about the plans for the org's future that they mentioned a new effort they were thinking of starting. This new effort immediately piqued my interest. It was related to work that I was currently doing, meant building something from scratch, and required creating many connections across the broader org. However, they already had a lead in mind for this effort, and they were thinking of kicking it off very soon.

I didn't know what to do. On the one hand, the manager I was very impressed with offered me a good spot on his org. I should have been happy about it. On the other hand, I kept thinking about this new opportunity and how it would have been perfect for me if they hadn't already picked the lead.

After days of back-and-forth with myself, really wanting to be involved in the new effort but fearing I might lose the original offer if I didn't just accept it at face value, I decided that I owed it to myself to let them know I cared more about the opportunity they didn't offer me than the one they did. In a well-crafted email I explained that I was very passionate about this new direction and wondered whether there might be a path for me to lead it. I realized it was a rude request (written very politely!), but I figured if I didn't at least ask, I definitely wouldn't get it. This led me to learn lesson number two.

Lesson 2: If opportunity doesn't knock, build a door. *Often the opportunities won't be there for you to pick from. Creating the right opportunities for yourself is critical for building the path that suits you.*

I received an email back saying they had thought it through, and if I was interested the new job was mine. I was ecstatic. There's nothing more rewarding than having your job be the thing you're passionate about. And knowing that I overcame my fears and asked for what I wanted made it even better.

Fast forward a couple of years: This effort grew from an initial idea to a team of five engineers. I grew to be a manager and took the responsibility of looking after people's personal growth in addition to driving the technical direction for the team.

At first, I had a very good handle on how to operate. Having built the product from the ground up, I knew it front and back and was able to dive into the details of any decision my team members were making. After a while though, my management and other responsibilities meant that I had less time for the details, and the deep understanding I had slowly drifted away. New additions to the code were quickly piling up. I didn't always manage to do code reviews, and there were topics that I wasn't the most knowledgeable on anymore. My solution was to work harder and make more time to get to the same level of familiarity I had before. As compelling as it may be, that solution is pretty much always the wrong one. Lesson number three is one that I learned the hard way and through advice from other managers who have gone through this process before.

Lesson 3: Make yourself redundant. *Your goal should always be to try and find the areas in which you're the bottleneck and make sure you are no longer that. Teach others how to do it and automate it every way you can. Only when you make yourself redundant in your current responsibilities will you have time to really focus on the important issues.*

I embraced that lesson and acted on it and have been operating from that place ever since. It sounds counterintuitive, as it literally means that you should be doing less, but the reality is that once you're truly successful at being redundant, new opportunities and responsibilities tend to show up and you start all over again.

At the time, making myself redundant meant growing my bench. I developed a couple of key people in the team to become the point of contact for technical decisions in their area of expertise and coached them on how to apply critical judgment on designs, how to determine the tasks for the next few months, and how to ensure quality code reviews. I was able to rely on them more and more and turned into a reviewer of their decisions rather than being the decision maker myself. With the extra time, I was able to focus much more on the strategic questions, set the product direction, and build partnerships and collaborations with other teams. This in turn made me a natural fit to quickly take on the leadership of another team we had collaborated with. Had I not taken the time to make myself redundant, this new opportunity to increase my scope and grow into a group manager would not have come at this time.

At this point in my career, I already knew that I liked management. I enjoyed working with people, seeing them succeed, and brainstorming ideas together. I knew that taking on management of another team—effectively tripling the size of my team—would be harder, but deep down I assumed it would be the same as this muscle I like to work out. I quickly realized that it wasn't as easy, and that management is *not* like riding a bike.

Lesson 4: What got you here, won't get you there. *Adapting yourself to the challenges is key.*

It turned out there's a big difference between managing a team when you're the most knowledgeable person in the team and coming in as a manager who knows the least on the team. Your sources for authority are very different and require a whole new set of skills, including confidence in your ability to lead the team even with that knowledge gap. After I took on the role and started managing the larger team, I had to redefine for myself what makes me a good manager. I had to reassert for myself that I *was* a good manager. It was a big jump and it took me quite a lot of "fake it till you make it" cycles to notice the small signs that I was actually contributing—people on the team who sought my advice, meetings where a conflict was resolved due to my decision-making, and collaborations that became fruitful because of the way I was building bridges with other parts of the org.

There were many times where my rudimentary knowledge in the details of the new team was actually a blessing. Bringing that "outsider" perspective, along with the bigger picture perspective, meant that I was able to ask questions about the most basic assumptions that the team was unable to see because they were deep into the details of it. I was able to shift the direction of the product, stop initiatives that were going on inertia but no longer made sense, and start new ones instead. I adapted to the role and realized that I was bringing a fresh perspective that was extremely valuable.

My career didn't end there. I went on to lead other and larger groups, took on more opportunities, and learned more skills that I continue to try and perfect. The lessons that I learned in these early years are still valid, and I apply them constantly in my career even today.

PART IV

MANAGERS

CHAPTER 20

Building Your Manager Persona

Despite her success in her current manager role, one of my mentees struggled to find a new position. Ella had several interviews and couldn't figure out why she wasn't getting hired. It got so bad that she was considering applying for a team lead position instead.

After searching unsuccessfully for a long time, Ella came to me for guidance. As we talked, we found several issues in the persona she was presenting during interviews. For example, there were spots where she lacked confidence or had holes in her story, as well as areas where she struggled to explain herself to the interviewers' satisfaction. For example, she was somewhat timid and soft spoken, and when she was asked how she would handle opinionated, passionate environments, she didn't give the interviewers confidence that she would manage it well. I explained that even if she had negative moments in her career, the important thing was being able to explain them in a positive light. She could tell her interviewer about her challenges; she just needed to also show what she learned from that experience.

I gave Ella a full list of questions to consider. By fleshing out those details, she built her own story. When she entered interviews after that, she had an agenda to guide the narrative to her benefit. When she was pressed on things like being soft spoken, she answered in a way that emphasized her confidence: she knew exactly what she believed in, what she didn't, how she worked, and how she handled problems.

Rather than changing her style, Ella owned it and knew how to share who she was and how she worked. Because she had a full narrative about herself, she felt more confident. Soon after, she succeeded in her job search and landed a new manager role.

This chapter provides the questions I asked Ella. By reflecting on these aspects of your manager persona, you can craft the story you tell potential interviewers. In addition, these questions will help you think about how you want to present yourself as a manager in your day-to-day interactions.

UNDERSTANDING YOUR MANAGER PERSONA

By "manager persona," I mean how you manage others and what you emphasize in your role: your main goals as a manager, your strengths and weaknesses, how you handle conflict, what you expect from direct reports, and so on. There are no right or wrong answers. The goal is simply for you to self-reflect and be honest with yourself about the kind of manager you are.

The following questions cover four main areas of your persona: personality, technology, development, and philosophy.

PERSONALITY

The personal aspect of your persona involves how you work as a manager: your style, your personality traits, your strengths and weaknesses. As you answer these questions, you'll likely identify areas where you are content with how you're showing up and others where you want to improve.

How do you present yourself? Your abilities? Your past achievements? Do you differentiate between when you accomplished something versus when your team accomplished something?

What are your biggest strengths? Are you a technological manager? Are you exceptionally skilled at managing people? Do you excel at building processes or creating order within your team? For example, I used to be a very technological-focused manager. Now I have more interest in the people and delivery side of management and less in the details of the code. I've chosen to focus on this aspect of management, and I look for companies that fit my abilities. Similarly, know your strengths and use them to your advantage.

What do you expect from a workplace? Remember that as much as the interviewer is testing you, you're also testing the company. Some mentees I've worked with tell me that they try to get accepted at a company without revealing their true personality. They hope to seem like a perfect fit, get the offer, and then decide about compatibility later. Don't approach interviewing this way. For one, you may come across as dishonest if you hold back. Second, you don't want to get a job at a company that doesn't work well with your personality.

When interviewing for a management position, you'll face difficult questions on the personal side as well as the technical. Speak truthfully about who you are. Remember: it's better to be rejected by a company that won't suit your needs well than to join it and be miserable. If you understand that you are more mild-mannered and easygoing, then you'll know you won't have an enjoyable work experience at a company with an aggressive culture, and you can end the process with that organization and move on.

When I was looking for a VP position, I had a call with a company's rep. She told me that they were looking for a VP who dreamt about technology at night.

"I don't dream about technology," I replied. "I dream about people who are happy and committed to their company and about delivering great products."

In the end, I didn't interview with this company. We had different dreams, so we weren't going to be a good fit. To make a decision like this, you have to know yourself: your dreams, your goals, and your priorities as a manager.

How do you talk about the "bumps" in your career—the less positive moments, like being fired? Learn how to talk about yourself confidently, no matter what has happened. This might take practice, so work through the bumps of your narrative with a friend or trusted colleague. Learn how to present that part of your story with confidence rather than fumbling. The other person can give you fresh eyes on how to present your complicated career moments. If you hesitate when asked a question about these bumps during an interview, make a mental note of the question so you can practice it again at home.

Is there anyone you want to base your manager style on? If so, notice how this person presents herself in various scenarios: How does she handle friendly conversation with direct reports? Unexpected problems? Conflict? Imagine how she speaks in each situation, practice on your own, and then be this kind of manager both in interviews and in everyday interactions.

What have you learned from your mistakes? Know how to explain why you made that choice and what you would do differently now that you've had that experience. Most interviews conducted at Facebook focus on failure; they want to know where you've had issues with coworkers, your team members, and your managers, and how you handled each situation. As someone who interviews managers, I also ask about failure.

What's a conflict you've had with either a manager or a colleague? As with your mistakes, be honest. Know how to explain what happened and how you handled the conflict, as well as the ultimate resolution. If you didn't achieve what you wanted, be able to explain why. Sharing this will show your interviewer how you handle hard situations.

TECHNOLOGY

Interviewers will ask about your technology experience and knowledge, so take time to think about these aspects of your career, whether you performed well or made mistakes. Consider the following questions as you self-reflect on the technology part of your persona.

What is the architecture of the product you worked on? Know how to draw the architecture of the product. What happened during production failures? Which services did you implement?

Which databases did you use and why? Which services talked with one another, and what technology did you use to enable that? When did you use queues? What kind of queues did you use?

How do you approach scaling issues? A great example to share would be one where you expected more customers or more data and realized you needed to scale your systems. Or perhaps you reduced the processing time of some calculations in your system so that the same number of resources can handle a bigger number of calculations.

How have you implemented change? Here, you can share about the design of a complicated feature that you led. Give examples of when you changed technology, including why you changed it and how you managed the change.

DEVELOPMENT (AGILE)

Agile allows you as a manager to implement more continual feedback, continuous integration, and continuous deployment. You're constantly developing your skills and knowledge, improving your cycle to develop features faster, receive better feedback, and grow overall. Build that cycle within the group of people you manage.

If you work solely on R&D, for example, then you're likely to become a good R&D manager. But if you truly understand the business—its goals, its vision, the roadmap—you become a much better manager overall because you can predict, plan, and direct better. You'll know how to measure performance better because you understand the true goals of the company. You'll become more than just a good R&D manager; you'll be an exceptional, well-rounded manager.

PRO TIP

Women who reach the manager level tend to stay focused on the details because they are afraid they'll lose their knowledge of the code. They also think staying in the details makes them a good manager. I've met women who have teams of twenty and still review each developer's code. Staying in the details like this can hold you back from being the best manager you can be. Remember: upper management isn't about the details.

Instead of micromanaging, stay focused on the bigger picture. Pay special attention to the future: the goals of the product, the goals of the company, and what your team needs to reach those goals. Learn to anticipate future needs: what might fail, how to fix it, when you will need more resources or team members. As part of your manager persona, move away from micromanaging and instead develop a big picture view.

I go even further. I make myself as disposable as possible, so that my team is almost 100 percent independent. My goal is to reach a place where they are a better team when I'm around, but they are also fully functional without me. This allows me to be involved in the company's future and strategy and anticipate whatever is needed to be anticipated.

How do you approach Agile? Agile is the primary approach used today for project management and software development. It helps teams deliver value by creating small, incremental development cycles, which allows for faster delivery. If you've worked with the Agile framework, then you likely have a preference for how it's set up. Be ready to share how you implemented it previously and where it did or didn't work.

If your new company doesn't set up its Agile system the same way you would, that's okay. In fact, I recommend that you avoid adjusting large structural components like length of sprints or standups in the beginning. You might fix processes so they are more streamlined, but if systems are working before you arrive, there's no reason to change them.

I knew a senior manager who immediately changed the tools and methodologies of his new company. For example, he changed sprints from two weeks to three weeks and measured them in points instead of days. In the process, he spent a lot of time fighting people who didn't like the fact that he was changing the systems they were used to. The end result was minimal improvement and lots of frustrated coworkers.

How do you measure the success of your team? Do you measure points in a sprint? Do you measure the number of bugs after the feature came out to the customer? Do you measure the performance of specific areas in your product? Do you measure how many times production broke down? How much downtime do you have, if any? Do you measure specific information, such as the amount of customer requests or data collected, relevant to your product?

For example, at one of my workplaces we measured the number of opened bugs after each sprint. At another, where our main business involved creating customer insights, we looked at how many customers opened our emails and used the insights we sent. To ensure that we provided real value through these emails, we analyzed how many customers took an action such as downloading the insight to their personal computer. When customers weren't reading, opening, or downloading our emails, we spoke with customer success to understand why our insights didn't interest the customer and how we could improve.

If you have an example like this that shows where R&D contributed to your company's success related to the product being used, use it in interviews. If you don't, think about ways you can create future examples like the ones mentioned earlier: implementing features that track open emails, downloaded insights, likes—or whatever is appropriate given the product your company is working on. Not only will such examples look good in interviews, but implementing them will give added value to your current company.

PHILOSOPHY

Your personal philosophy dictates how you lead in every aspect of your job. It touches every decision you make and every goal you set. Be sure to approach your manager role with thoughtfulness, and consider your personal big picture goals and beliefs.

Did you ever build a group from scratch? Did you come to a group that needed restructuring? What did you do? What did you change and why? How did it fit the company goals and how did you empower people?

How do you manage people? What is your management style? Are you a friendly manager or focused on hierarchy? Do you share dilemmas with people who report to you, or do you make decisions yourself? How do you manage your team leads? Do you tell them what to do? Direct them? Ask them questions? Allow them to make mistakes?

How in touch are you with the people who are not reporting to you directly? Do you meet one on one with people who report to your team leads? Do you have regular group meetings? Do you lead architectural discussions, or do you let someone senior from your team do it?

How do you handle yourself in various relationships? How do you handle yourself with colleagues, both during day-to-day tasks and in the event of a dispute? How do you manage conflicts? How do you achieve goals when you have different opinions? What is the best way to manage you?

What challenges have you faced as a manager? What did you learn from them? Have you fired employees? How did you handle that? Did you make mistakes—in firing employees and elsewhere? What did you learn from those mistakes?

How did you approach a new management position? What is the first thing you changed or implemented? Why did you do that? For example, I tend to enter a new job first by observing the situation around me. I'll wait until I see something that is causing issues and then I'll make a change. That way, I don't start off with resentful team members who feel like I'm making unnecessary changes. Additionally, I make sure to have clear, strong reasons for the change. Compare this to a manager I once had, who immediately changed a tool to one he was more comfortable with, even though everyone on his team preferred the tool they were already using. I don't think his change was totally wrong; he used a more modernized tool and that was good. However, it was a big change with only medium value that made a lot of people angry. When you make changes, consider all of the impacts of your decision and then choose the ones to implement.

How do you work with the Product team? If you worked in different companies or groups within the same organization, what was effective? What wasn't? What would you change about your relationship with this group and your interactions with them? Do you do post-mortems—in-depth debriefings after a big failure? If so, how do you handle them?

PREPARE YOUR ANSWERS

There isn't one right manager persona. The key is to reflect on and build your own. Know what is important to you, how you work best, how you handle conflict and mistakes, how you handle code and technology—all of the topics just discussed. Taking time to answer these questions for yourself will prepare you for your next interview, and it will also help you become comfortable with who you are as a manager once you're in that role.

If you read some of these questions and realized you need to work on certain areas, then do it. No matter where you are in your career, start reviewing and answering these questions now. Doing so will increase your confidence and set you up to be the manager you truly want to be.

IN HER WORDS: HILA NOGA

I understand machines better than I understand human beings. Or at least, this is what I always used to tell myself. Like many in our industry, I was a nerdy child. Books, studies, and good grades were easy for me, but the rest was a different story. I never fit in. I always seemed to say the wrong thing, behave in an odd manner, break some unwritten rule, and inadvertently hurt someone's feelings.

I joined the army as a software developer, hoping to bury myself in logic, structure, and abstractions that would shield me from the chaotic and perplexing world of human relationships, which is why I was completely baffled when I was offered a teaching role after my basic training course. I was obviously not the right person for the job, so naturally I had to take it. After all, **what new things would I learn about myself by making only obvious choices?** This became a guiding principle in my career.

They say that in order to get ahead you have to know what you want to be in five to ten years and plan your way toward it. I rarely knew where I wanted to go. Instead, I opted to build my career opportunistically as a series of local choices, each aimed at increasing the challenge I take on myself, making things more interesting for me, or introducing some other meaningful change into my life. My rule of thumb for assessing opportunities is that **if a role sounds like it's tailored for you, it's probably too small for you.**

It turned out my bewilderment at the teaching offer wasn't entirely misplaced as, at the age of eighteen, I had absolutely zero ability to understand and do what was expected of me. I got myself kicked out of commander training with a discharge note saying that I am unfit for leadership. To this day I am not 100 percent sure what I did to earn such a fine evaluation, but at the time I was sure of one thing: giving up wasn't an option. The day after my discharge, I cheered my friends at their graduation ceremony, and two days later I joined the next round of the course with the same staff that thought so highly of me the first time. Naturally, I hadn't learned much from my first experience. Naturally, my staff didn't magically change their opinion of me, and naturally, I almost got myself kicked out again.

The second time around I did get a metaphorical A for effort, though, and I got to shake my commander's hand with teary eyes as my friends cheered me at my own graduation ceremony.

But things still weren't perfect—as one might expect, my teaching role didn't go very smoothly, and it took me a couple more rough years before I realized that I am the common denominator in all my turbulent relationships. With this realization, I set out to debug my people skills. I started breaking down all my interactions and analyzing them. I read books about psychology, social skills, and management. I enlisted the help of professionals, mentors, and trusted friends. I observed others, took notes, experimented, and drew conclusions. I made charts.

Eventually I did manage to get better at people-ing. I learned how to communicate with more care, to see others' perspectives, and to recover relationships, and it paid off in my career. My colleagues started valuing me not only as an engineer but also as a person. The people I managed seemed to do well. Through my process, I discovered that often our ability to own our mistakes and shortcomings and to make an honest effort to fix them is more important than not making any mistakes in the first place. The latter is an unachievable ideal, the former is something one can work toward.

To my surprise, at some point people started coming to me for professional and interpersonal advice. It so happened that through my own difficulty, I managed to come up with non-obvious ways to debug interactions, and non-trivial conclusions about human interactions at large. These then became tools that I could pass on. **In a sense, my difficulty became a distinctive strength of mine.**

From a person who was deemed unfit to lead, I became a person who naturally gravitates toward leadership roles.

GIVING YOURSELF PERMISSION

I find a lot of us have a hard time imagining an ambitious future for ourselves as it requires a level of self-confidence and "chutzpah" that not everyone feels comfortable with. For us to make the leap, sometimes we need a friend or manager with a keen eye who sees in us something we cannot see in ourselves. The role of CTO certainly wasn't something that I envisioned for myself. It was a friend, Youval Vaknin, who told me that he thought I could be great in this role, for me to consider it, and for that I am ever grateful. This is one of the ways in which the people in our lives can make us or break us, and why I think we should always surround ourselves with smart, kind, and supportive people.

I entered the role with a great deal of anxiety. I had never even seen a seasoned CTO operate, let alone worked with one before I became one myself, and I wasn't entirely sure I had what it takes to do the job. Since I couldn't find a "CTO school," I scrambled around trying to figure out my responsibilities and did the thing that seemed to make the most sense at any given moment. Looking back, I would tell my younger self to not stress so much about her mistakes. Everyone makes mistakes. She also ended up doing a lot of the right things.

This is not unique neither to me nor to the CTO position. We tend to think about roles as a strict list of qualifications and responsibilities we must fit ourselves into, but it's been my observation that more often we shape our roles around us by doing more of the things we excel at, the things we are moved to do, the things that set us apart, and the things that allow us to drive the most impact, and **our roles are shaped by the unique combination of qualities we possess rather than the other way around.**

After a couple of years of CTO-ing, I was moved to create something of my own as an entrepreneur. Fueled by my previous experience, I no longer needed someone else to imagine my future for me or felt the need to get anyone's approval. **This time I could give myself permission.** I consider this experience one of the most challenging yet fulfilling things I did in my career.

FINDING MEANING

My entrepreneurial journey ended abruptly when I became ill and had to leave my company in order to give myself time to recover. I returned to the job market before I was completely well and aimed for individual contributor roles in established companies because I didn't want to take on the responsibility of leading an effort when I wasn't physically well enough to deliver.

Those of us who are very career driven tend to get very attached to it. When I co-founded my company, I gradually shed all other activities in order to focus on my work, and without noticing, I wrapped my entire identity around it. Consequently, when I had to leave, I found myself harboring a void that was hard to fill. I had always imagined that, if I needed to, I could return to doing the things I enjoyed before, but when I tried to do this, I realized I had changed in ways that made it difficult to find the same kind of meaning I used to find in them. This was one of the hardest lessons I had to learn, that no matter how driven and focused you are, **always have multiple things going on in your life so that if something falls through, you will have a safety net.**

And so I was forced to stop and ask myself how I define success. To a large extent, I think we have a choice about the values we lead our lives according to, and with this choice we can set ourselves up for happiness or for a great deal of misery. Throughout most of my life I either didn't have a clear notion of what success was to me and felt that I lacked direction, or I had a very specific idea of what it should look like, which left me frustrated and upset when things didn't go exactly as I had imagined.

These days I am fulfilling my thirteen-year-old self's dreams by trying out a research-oriented role. With this move, it feels like I ran out of items from my bucket list of directions to explore. In the explore vs. exploit game of life, I spent most of my time in explore mode, but sometimes our strategy ceases to serve us, and when this happens, we are allowed to rethink it. I believe my next move should be changing modes and finding a goal that is bigger than myself to work toward with people I love. I still don't know where this new road will lead me, but I'm excited to find out.

ON LABELS: AN EPILOGUE

It came as no surprise to me that I got an autism diagnosis in my thirties. The difficulties I had at the beginning of my career were typical of autistic people: I felt that I was born into this world without the book of social rules everyone else seemed to be equipped with, and my path was to write my own copy of the book, in my own language.

These days when I tell people about my diagnosis, the most common response I get is disbelief, but if I had been given a label at a younger age, I doubt I would have had the opportunity to transcend it. Over time I learned not to see it as the thing that defines the limit of my abilities, but as a lens through which I can examine my individual strengths and weaknesses and identify where I can easily excel and where I need to be compassionate with myself and spend more time in order to push myself forward. **Essentially, it is my roadmap to succeeding while being myself.**

CHAPTER 21

Recruiting and Retaining Employees

I was working as the VP of R&D for a startup company when it finally grew large enough to bring on an additional software engineer. Since I had a few seniors, I felt like the team could handle supporting and guiding a junior, so I recruited a junior software engineer from a prestigious university. We had amazing candidates and eventually picked someone who seemed like she could work independently. She quickly went from handling small tasks to taking on more and more responsibilities. Overall, she was a fantastic recruit.

You may not be a VP yet, but recruiting is still part of your job description as a manager. You are responsible for finding the right people for your team and then doing what you can to retain them. In this chapter, we'll discuss the best strategies for recruiting, negotiating salaries and benefits, and handling raises.

RECRUITING SUCCESSFULLY

Recruiting good people for your team is more art than science. On paper, some engineers may have all the needed skills and experience, but their personality and work style do not fit with your team. You want to build a team that has a variety of abilities *and* works together in harmony.

Finding the right fit can be challenging under "normal" conditions, but it's even more difficult when the industry experiences a hiring bubble. When market changes result in a higher demand for technology, tech companies—and especially startups—receive an influx of money, so companies start more projects and need to hire more engineers. But since everyone is in the same position, finding enough engineers to fill the available positions is not easy. An accelerated hiring need like this occurred in the early 2000s, and it's occurring again as of this writing in 2022.[32]

No matter what the hiring climate is like right now, the following strategies will ensure that you explore all of your options for finding the best talent for your team.

A FRIEND BRINGS A FRIEND

In Hebrew, there's a saying: "a friend brings a friend." Essentially, this means that people you already know can help you find more people—the same idea behind networking and employee referral programs across the globe. One of the best ways to recruit, especially in hiring bubbles, is to encourage your current employees to help you network for new positions. You can even reach out to people you've previously worked with at other companies. If

---

[32] Nally C., "Will Software Engineering Bubble Burst?" *McNally Institute*, April 9, 2022, https://www.mcnallyinstitute.com/will-software-engineering-bubble-burst/.

you had a good relationship with someone, see if she would be interested in working with you again.

RECRUIT OFFSHORE

If you can't find local talent, consider recruiting offshore. Global engineering services outsourcing is a fast-growing industry, forecasted to be worth over $2,000 billion from 2021 to 2027.[33] I've personally worked with skilled engineers from countries like Ukraine, Poland, Russia, and Georgia.

If you're interested in recruiting offshore, start by looking for recommended agencies. If you can't find any, start researching online. See how fast the agencies provide you with interviews. When conducting interviews, treat the process the same as you would in your own country. Start with one agency and then branch out if need be. If you're able to work in your same time zone, do it.

When you hire outside your country, you'll often work with a specific placement agency to find developers. Once you've found an agency that you work well with, it's easier to bring on more people through that same agency.

One benefit of offshore recruiting is that you can grow your team much faster. Let's say I manage a small startup in Israel that has eight developers, six Israeli and two Ukrainian. If my company raises enough money to grow the team to twenty developers, I can build up the team much faster by recruiting in both countries. You might also find skilled talent at a cheaper price when you hire offshore.

---

33 "Engineering Services Outsourcing Market Size Worth US $3,803.21 Bn by 2027," Astute Analytica, January 19, 2022, https://www.prnewswire.com/news-releases/engineering-services-outsourcing-market-size-worth-us-3-803-21-bn-by-2027--cagr-17-7--astute-analytica-301463690.html.

> **PRO TIP**
>
> When you hire people from other countries, you need to work harder to create a cohesive team. You can do this by doing dailies and tasks together and by working in tandem with video communication like Zoom as much as possible. Make sure that your offshore team is truly aligned with all tasks and information and that they feel like supported members of the group.
>
> On the local end, explain that the offshore engineers and developers should be treated the same as any other team member. While they aren't able to attend company happy hours, they should be included as much as possible—through dailies, equity in task sharing, and code reviews. I recommend having integrated teams, where some members are local and others are offshore. By managing your team, both local and offshore, and making them all feel like they're a part of something, you become a great manager.

INTERVIEWS

In this section, we'll discuss the technical part of interviewing. For help with personal interviews, refer back to Chapter 9.

When the market is balanced, I recommend giving candidates home tests to help evaluate their abilities to write code. However, unless your company is one of the FAANG organizations, more experienced engineers won't go through the process of a home test because they can find an organization that doesn't require it.

Instead of a home test, have candidates complete a significant system design question and a coding question such as LeetCode during the actual interview. This might involve having them design the architecture of Twitter or Wikipedia. Additionally, you can have them write up the architecture they used at a former company. While you'll know less about the candidate than if they were to do a home test, it makes it easier to recruit them overall, as many candidates—especially seniors—will walk away at the mention of a home test.

ARRANGE A MEETING

As a candidate gets closer to the end of the interview process, have them talk with the people they would work with on a day-to-day basis. It doesn't have to be everyone; just select people on the team. Some companies will even initiate lunches with candidates to make sure their personalities mesh well with the rest of the team. This allows both you and the candidate to confirm there are no red flags in terms of the new employee meshing well with the team.

COMPLEMENTARY RECRUITS

Look for candidates who will complement your style. I don't like details or tracking many tasks. When I look for employees, I search for people who will do well in areas I don't. I also prefer to work with enthusiastic people who have a strong drive and like to fix problems. You have to know yourself in order to know who you need on your team.

CONSIDER ALL OPTIONS

Be open to recruiting people who are culturally diverse. In Israel, for example, I've managed extremely Jewish Orthodox women who had specific needs, such as never being alone in a room with a man and eating kosher. Other companies decided not to consider these women because of their needs, but I found them to be great employees who contributed a lot of power to the team. If you're open to all types of people, you will find extremely skilled programmers in previously untapped areas.

SALARIES, BONUSES, AND RAISES

As a manager, money matters like salaries, bonuses, and raises are now your responsibility. Here are some points to consider.

INITIAL OFFERS

During the process of hiring new engineers, salary, benefits, and bonuses will always come up as part of the discussion. If your company is in a position to offer top dollar, great. That's a selling point in your favor. If not, you should know how to sell your company, management, and group with benefits beyond salary. Have a good story about why someone's career will benefit from working at your company, even if you aren't offering the highest salary on the market.

HANDLING RAISES

I once worked with a developer who felt like he deserved a large raise. Alex's previous manager told him he did a great job, so he was under the impression that he was an extremely talented engineer who was severely underpaid. I, personally, was very displeased with his performance.

Though it was difficult, I explained to Alex why he hadn't earned the raise. I gave him examples of when he didn't finish projects on time, when the quality of his work was low, and when he neglected aspects of his projects. Alex left my office frustrated, both by my feedback and by the fact that I didn't give him a raise.

The manager before me did this engineer a disservice in telling him he was doing well. Even though it can be difficult, part of your job is being upfront with your employees about their performance.

In big organizations, the process of evaluating raises and bonuses is very standardized, based on process and measurements. Often smaller companies don't have the same level of organized process. Even if you work in a smaller company, you still want to be competitive on the market front. You also want to be fair to your employees. Some managers only give money to those who repeatedly ask for raises, but I recommend you look beyond the loudest voices. See who is truly underpaid and offer her a raise. Find ways to treat raises equitably.

During hiring bubbles, companies struggle to retain employees as much as they struggle to hire them. Knowing there is competition, if engineers aren't getting a raise from their current employers, they will often look elsewhere to make more money. Some companies end up giving employees huge salary raises to keep the talent, sometimes giving everyone in the R&D department a raise.

Hiring and training new employees is expensive and time consuming, so it's worth your while to incentivize employees to stay if possible. Raises are the most obvious way to do this, if the money is available.

Most companies handle raises by giving managers a lump sum based on their team's annual earnings. As the manager, you then have to distribute that amount throughout your group. Imagine that you are given a cake to divide among your team. If you give one person a larger piece of cake, that means another person will end up with a smaller slice. If it's an option at your company, you can balance any decision you make through bonuses.

When you give out raises, imagine that everyone's salaries are hung up on a wall for all to see. Make sure that you feel okay about each salary as it compares to the others, and that your employees would feel okay too. Know how to explain any discrepancies. If you're not embarrassed by the idea of everyone seeing each other's salaries, you're probably right on target.

Sometimes, you will make decisions surrounding salaries that you aren't proud of. For example, you might have someone in your group who earns very little for her skill level. Perhaps she negotiated poorly when she started, so now she's underpaid. You might want to give her a large raise to compensate for that, and even resent the fact that you can't because her raise will come out of the budget for the whole group. It's important to do something, even if you can only partly fix the gap, and then keep her in mind for a bonus or other benefits, like going to a prestigious conference.

BEYOND SALARY

Make sure your employees are committed to you for other reasons too.

Some companies simply won't or can't be competitive with salary, both when it's initially offered to a recruit and when it comes time for raises. When this happens, they'll try to stand out in other ways. Some companies make products that benefit humanity. They hope that people will want to work for them because they share the company's desire to do good for the world. Other companies pride themselves on a great work culture and attract and maintain employees that way.

Another way to retain employees is offering opportunities for personal development. One strategy is to encourage your employees to speak at conferences, write blogs, or contribute code to open-source products on the company's dime. Helping employees grow can be risky because it increases their desirability to other companies. However, if you don't allow your employees to work on personal development, they might leave anyway. Better to take a chance and invest in employees' goals by providing them with opportunities to advance in skills and knowledge.

If you are looking to add a new team lead or another senior position, consider promoting someone from your own group. Even if it means working with someone less experienced and less senior, you can support them if they have the right potential. Your employees will also appreciate seeing someone promoted from inside the company. If you bring people from the outside for a larger role like team lead, people become discouraged about their own chances for promotion. Employees are also more likely to stay if they see that getting a promotion internally is a real possibility. If an employee wants to climb the ladder but doesn't see a viable route, they'll likely leave.

If someone is threatening to leave if you don't give them a bigger raise, you need to pause. Decide if the person is worth keeping; not everyone is. If they're making a big deal about it, the best choice might be to let them go and use the money to reward other people who are worth keeping. Even if you give the complainer a raise, they might not think it's enough and leave anyway. Better to invest your limited funds elsewhere.

OWN YOUR DECISIONS

When it comes to recruits, salaries, and raises, remember this: not everybody will like your decisions. If you've considered everything and know the risks (i.e., people leaving), then own your decision. I say, if you want everyone to like you, sell ice cream.

Another key aspect of your role as manager is that you will now be supervising people who also supervise others. We'll discuss this next.

CHAPTER 22

Managing Other Managers

When I was a manager, I had a team lead named Noah who supervised a team of five software engineers, including Samuel. When he actually did his job, Samuel was a brilliant and fast engineer. But the rest of the time, he could be quite immature. He often showed up late without explanation, disappeared without telling anyone, and worked fewer hours than the rest of the team.

Noah knew he needed to talk to Samuel, but he struggled with confrontation. He disliked setting boundaries or making difficult decisions. Despite his behavior issues, Samuel was a nice person overall, which made it even harder for Noah to confront him.

Rather than stepping in myself, I worked with Noah so he could build his own skills around difficult conversations. We talked through all of the issues with Samuel and how to address them. Through our coaching session, Noah recognized that he was afraid of people not liking him. Once he identified that, he started working on his mindset and then set up a meeting to talk with Samuel.

Unfortunately, Noah went too easy on Samuel and nothing changed. He skirted around the actual issues, so his feedback came off as suggestions, not actual problems to fix. He needed to explain exactly what was wrong with Samuel's behavior.

On our next one on one, Noah and I discussed the issue again. I coached him on how to deliver his feedback in a more assertive, direct manner. Noah practiced saying things like, "You need to come on time." "Tell me if you're going to be late." "You are expected to work during normal business hours." "If you finish a project early, tell me so that I can give you your next task."

I pretended to be Samuel and was purposefully difficult so Noah could practice dealing with pushback. "What's the problem?" I asked. "I finish everything before everyone and I'm really good. Why do I need to change?"

Then Noah practiced responding firmly and directly, "The problem is you are not reliable. When you don't communicate, you leave me in the dark about problems. If you're bored, I can easily give you more work, but you have to tell me."

After our meeting, Noah spoke with Samuel. This time, Samuel understood the problem and started improving.

A few months passed and then Samuel began to regress. This time, Noah handled the discussion on his own without my coaching.

As a team lead, you manage software engineers. As a manager, however, you supervise team leads like Noah who are also managing others. In this role, you are a coach and mentor, as well as a manager. I could have talked to Samuel myself, but that wouldn't have helped Noah's growth. By having these meetings, I coached Noah to be a better leader himself.

In this chapter, we'll discuss how to give feedback and help managers work through problems with their own teams.

MANAGER AS COACH

As seen in the way I worked with Noah, coaching your managers involves challenging them to have difficult conversations and give direct feedback to help their team. As a manager, you need to understand the goals of your company, group, and product. Once you understand the bigger picture and communicate it to the team leads under you, you can give them independence. Let them manage with their own style and accept that they might manage differently than you do.

Managing other managers requires trust. You need to let go of the details and allow them to lead in their own style. Listen to the challenges they're facing. Ask questions and ensure that they're learning from the problems and mistakes that arise. As I did with Noah, take time to coach them in coaching their own people.

Evaluating individual contributors, that is, people without direct reports, is easier because they have their own goals and measurements not dependent on how their people perform. When you evaluate managers, however, there's an added layer of complexity because you're not simply measuring the individual's accomplishments but the accomplishments of her team.

> **PRO TIP**
>
> When working with newer managers, attend their team meetings, their architecture meetings, and the interviews they conduct. During these meetings, simply listen. Anytime you're in front of a team lead's people, give her positive feedback. In private, correct and guide her as necessary.

When your manager fails—when people on her team make mistakes, or when a project misses a deadline or has lots of bugs once it goes live—don't approach managers with the attitude of, "Why didn't you succeed?" Instead, ask how you can help them succeed in the future.

The newer a team lead is to managing, the more you should be involved, but not to the point of micromanaging. Giving feedback, sharing where to grow, and pointing out successes are all parts of being a good manager. You get into micromanaging territory when you do someone's role, like talking to a direct report for them. Instead, focus on coaching and mentoring them to take care of the situation. As you climb the hierarchy, aim to become less concerned with giving the right answers and more focused on asking the right questions to help others come up with the answers and make decisions. Give team leads space to work with interfaces on their own. Take the time to check in with them regularly, ask them how they approach problems, and follow up with them to see how they're handling their roles. The key part here is that the team lead is working with the interfaces themselves—not you.

As a manager, you probably supervise two to four team leads. I recommend holding weekly management meetings where you bring together all of your team leads so they can help each other.

Allow space for the team leads to share what they're working on, bring up issues, and brainstorm ideas and solutions. Use this time to sync up as a group. For example, I once worked with two team leads who were struggling with the skills of developers on their own teams. When we discussed the issue in one of our meetings, we realized we could swap the two developers in question. This solution solved both team leads' problems as they now had people with the needed skills and it helped out everyone in the process.

Every two weeks or so, hold a meeting with everyone in your team. If the time allows, have every team lead and software engineer share what they've been working on. Discuss the roadmap, new customers, the goals of the company, and achievements. Have people present their successful features. You can also ask someone to prepare a lecture for the group so everyone learns together.

MANAGER AS FACILITATOR

When you manage team leads, you have an indirect impact on their people. My suggestion is to make that impact more direct—not to undermine the team leads' authority, but to have a better understanding of the overall health of your team and each individual on it.

To do this, schedule one-on-ones with those you aren't managing directly—I make time for these meetings every two to three months. I once managed a team totaling forty people, and I made sure to have individual meetings with everyone in the group. While it took a long time to meet with everyone, the result was well worth it. I learned about the group members' day-to-day activities; who was happy and who wasn't; what processes, procedures, and parts of the code were working (and which weren't);

where there was conflict; who believed in the company; and what problems existed with other groups. Usually, I didn't keep problems between us; I made it an open conversation. When there was conflict, I'd ask to speak with the team lead so we could work toward a solution together.

Managing managers involves more coaching than dictating. Though you should train your team leads, you shouldn't treat them like children. When you're a manager, your direct reports are quite senior themselves and should be treated that way. After all, they're working their way up the ladder just like you.

The last section of this book covers the top rung on the development side of engineering: VP of R&D.

PART V

VPS OF R&D

CHAPTER 23

Entering the VP Position

Maya was the VP of R&D at a company that was losing customers. Everyone assumed that they left because the competition was cheaper. Maya created a feedback form for departing clients and realized that customers weren't leaving because of the price point but because they disliked certain behaviors of the system. Customer success had been hearing the complaints, but they hadn't responded to them adequately. Maya's work helped Product and R&D better understand the problems and come up with solutions, which reduced customer churn as a result. While this was completely outside of her responsibilities, Maya ended up helping out the organization in an outstanding way.

* * *

In her position as VP, Leah wasn't responsible for monitoring customer calls, but she took it on herself to do this. In particular, she tracked how fast customers received answers for their problems. Looking at the information, she discovered that during the weekend, customers dealt with long response times, often waiting three days before getting an answer. In response, Leah created an on-call system to cover the weekends. Customer satisfaction went up after she implemented it.

* * *

In her role as VP, Talia received a complicated feature request from sales. Knowing the feature would take a long time, she went back and looked at conversation recordings and heard the specifics of the clients' wants from the product. When she looked at the information, Talia realized that she could create a far simpler feature that would give customers the same result. Talia checked in with sales and worked to create the simpler feature. The customer signed, and Talia excelled beyond her job description to serve them.

* * *

At one company, I created and tracked analytics to see how customers used the product and realized they were creating an extra step in order to use the product the way they wanted to: they collected the data from the product and then created their own reports from it. We then developed a feature to create a report for them every morning. It increased their usage of our product, which was a huge plus because it meant they were more likely to stay loyal. Rather than doing all of the work manually as the customer, they could filter and create an automatic report. It saved them about 80 percent of the time they previously spent creating that report daily.

* * *

As these four stories show, the VP of R&D is in a unique position to bring value to her company. She can analyze the situation and take the initiative to try different tactics in a way she couldn't as team lead or manager.

This chapter provides an overview of what's involved in the VP of R&D position, starting with the process of attaining this role.

BECOMING VP OF R&D

When you're looking to become a VP of R&D, one of the most important ways to prepare for the role is to know your manager persona. You also need a certain level of maturity. You need to be proactive, to not take things personally, to work less with ego, to not get offended, and to be confident. Simply put, you need to have your shit together.

Depending on your situation, you might be promoted or hired externally to this position. Often, you'll be a director at a larger company and then hired on as a VP of R&D at a smaller startup. This is the route I took.

The interview process for this position is far less technical than any previous roles we've discussed. It feels more like a date: you're sharing your success stories, how you approach being the VP of R&D, and if you fit, they'll take you. It's a much more personal process, focused on attitude, management skills, style, and chemistry.

You'll rarely be tested on the technical side of things when you're brought on for this role, as often the company won't have a more senior position that knows the technical aspects of software engineering. While it's uncommon, they might bring in someone from outside to help interview you.

Everything that we've discussed so far related to other management positions is still relevant here—you'll still be implementing one-on-ones, planning timelines, and considering company strategy—but you will be executing these tasks on a much larger scale and from a much higher, broader point of view. Two chapters in particular will help as you enter this new level of management: Chapter 17, on roles and responsibilities, and Chapter 20, on building your manager persona.

Along with scope, the main difference from your previous management positions is that as VP of R&D, you are now 100 percent alone in your decision-making. You are responsible for scale and processes, structure and restructure, relationship with product, the quality of the production; it's all on you. As a result, you need to have a much clearer understanding of the organization as a whole and the product you are working on. You need to be able to solve more complicated problems, understand different structures for your group, and implement the right one for the purposes of your organization. You are also solely responsible for reflecting the needs of development to the CEO and the others at the C-suite level.

This all might sound intimidating, but if you have come so far, I am sure you are up for the challenge. And I am not alone: someone believed in you and promoted you or recruited you for this VP position. Take a deep breath and "woman up." You can do this!

Let's dive into some of your new responsibilities.

UNDERSTAND THE STRUCTURE

One of the biggest differences from your previous roles is that now you are expected to understand the big picture of the organization at all levels. You need to understand customer success, sales, and your customers' needs very well. This is different from managing the other departments, which you shouldn't try to do. Rather, you're seeing how R&D fits into the bigger picture.

In general, you might be hired as a VP in one of two types of businesses: a newer startup or a large established organization.

Often, startups have two founders. The more business-oriented founder often becomes the CEO, while the more technological founder becomes the CTO. In some cases, the CTO will have good-enough management skills and manage R&D successfully with all sizes of engineering groups. In my experience, however, when the engineering team hits around seven people, the startup needs someone with more than good-enough skills. They need someone who knows how to run processes like Agile and sprints, and who knows product definitions and how to plan for clear deliverables. At the beginning of a startup, the focus is on getting things done quick and dirty, doing whatever is needed, and meeting small sales demands. It's inevitably messy, which isn't bad, but at some point, order needs to come. Around this time, the founders will consider bringing on a VP of R&D.

Depending on the startup, you'll report to the CTO or the CEO. I prefer reporting to the CEO because I want to bring my own voice and management style to the role. In addition, if you report to the CTO, you aren't necessarily included on the management team and thus have a position that is lower than the rest of the VPs. In my opinion, reporting to the CTO is only worthwhile if you want to be more hidden, or if you want someone to have your back and pave the way for you. If you prefer this more discreet role, you might not be ready to be a VP.

If you were hired as VP of R&D at a large company, it's likely for one of two reasons: either you are replacing a former VP, or the company is expanding the organizational structure and creating a new VP position.

BE PREPARED TO SOLVE PROBLEMS

Whether you're hired by a startup or an established organization, you're often recruited because problems need to be solved. I've never heard of someone entering a VP position to discover nothing but smooth sailing and well-managed employees. Instead, you'll likely end up finding instances of poor management, inefficient processes, or a lack of personal responsibility. Solving these problems is part of your job as VP of R&D, so expect it from the beginning.

When you're hired, you'll learn the product as well as the problems relevant to the product. Start by observing. Watch everything; question everything—not just for the sake of argument, but rather to understand the company. Ask people what is or isn't working. This again depends on the size of the company, but I recommend interviewing as many people in your department as you can. I've worked with groups of around forty people, and I made sure to meet with every one of them. As you talk with more people, you get more perspectives and understand the business better, which will inform your decisions as VP.

As the VP of R&D, you have to understand the business. Speak with the senior managers of sales, customer success, and product. Understand where the company is headed, the vision for the company, where the company will grow, and how R&D should answer these needs. Understand the strengths and weaknesses of the company.

As you do this, start to figure out what R&D should prioritize. What can't be given up on? What can't be skipped? For example, if you're a medical startup with software online in the operating room, you can't have your product fail during surgery. It needs to be available at all times. You need to implement the technology so that it supports this priority. Additionally, your product should be well tested for critical components so it never fails from bugs or problems in the code.

In contrast, if your company develops a product that collects data and provides customer insight, your main challenge is handling the scale of your customer's data. You need to be ready for the next level in case your company signs an increasing number of customers. For this structure, you don't need to prioritize 100 percent functioning like you do for a medical product. Instead, you need to focus on monitoring data and knowing the trends of the data amounts.

Still another scenario would be a product bringing technology into old-fashioned areas such as insurance, law, or food tech. Often, your priority here is creating a usable, pretty straightforward user experience, rather than scale or 100 percent availability.

As the leader of development, mapping the product and its priorities helps you build and structure your group, production, and goals.

DIFFERENT DEVELOPMENT STRUCTURES

In the past, software development was split into different teams for backend, frontend, mobile, QA, and database experience. When you needed a feature, teams worked together to execute it across the different areas. This was a difficult and often messy task if the teams worked poorly together. They needed to synchronize all aspects, trying to balance resources to fit every feature.

In 2012 Spotify introduced the squad model and changed the software engineering world.

Under the squad model, teams work independently. Each team implements all parts of a specific feature or area, with people belonging to the squad responsible for product definition, backend, frontend, and any other skill needed to complete the team's tasks. The squad is 100 percent self-sufficient. This way, teams don't have to wait for other teams to give them resources.

The squad model creates autonomy and independence by letting features be developed inside a team. Additionally, it allows for scaling each engineering group. You can have many steps, processes, and teams that work independently while also communicating with each other, all of which increases innovation, productivity, and accountability. As a result, product quality improves.

When an organization transitions to squads, the culture shifts. The company's environment becomes less top-down and more collaborative. For example, someone can be a squad lead but not necessarily a team lead, or the squad lead of one group and team lead of a different group. This kind of culture shift is a positive thing, but it can also be difficult. People might have objections or struggle to understand how their new roles fit into the big picture. People need time to adjust to new concepts.

Companies customize the squad model to fit their own needs and internal goals—from the number of squads, to who leads squads, to the overall structure, and beyond. Depending on the company, they may or may not use team leads within the structure. When this happens, the squad is about features while team leads help with engineers' personal development.

A prerequisite to implementing the squad model is a modular architecture. If you are working on a monolith, you won't be able to implement a squad model because teams will step on each other's toes. However, please also remember that if you have a monolith architecture, it's advised to start changing that because of so many reasons, that implementing squads is the least of your problems. More about breaking a monolith in Chapter 26.

There are six common structures within the squad model, and the VP of R&D oversees them all. The first one is the most common in R&D:

- **Squads** tend to be six to twelve people. Each squad focuses on a specific feature area and a specific mission. Usually they have an Agile coach for support, as well as a product owner who provides guidance and is responsible for timelines and delegation of tasks. The team decides internally which Agile methodology, for example, Scrum or Kanban, to use.
- **Tribes** are composed of multiple squads that coordinate with one another on the same feature area. Small startups implementing the squad model typically only have one or

two squads and therefore don't need tribes. Large software groups tend to have a few tribes. Usually a tribe is 40 to 150 people. Each tribe has a lead. Sometimes the lead will have a title like VP of R&D or Director of R&D.
- **Chapters** are made up of specialists from different squads within a tribe who talk to each other and align on best practices.
- **Guilds** are similar to chapters, but they consist of specialists across the entire organization instead of solely within a tribe.
- **Trios** consist of a tribe lead, product lead, and design lead.
- **Alliances** are only implemented in huge organizations—usually at least five hundred people. When tribes need to work together to accomplish a goal, an alliance combines tribe trios to work together and ensure that tribes collaborate on larger goals.

Small- and medium-sized companies typically implement squads and guilds. If the company is small, there's no difference between a chapter and a guild. Again, companies will customize these roles to fit their own needs and size.

Some new VPs of R&D arrive at small organizations without strict structures. In order for the startup to grow, the VP might decide to implement the squad model within the organization. Often, someone within the company will suggest that they start using squads. Change is hard, and mess from change is inevitable. Embrace it.

If you help a company convert to the squad model, you can put on your resume that you've implemented squads. This is a huge achievement.

OBSERVE, THEN ACT

When you get started on your first VP job, don't jump in right away with grand plans for customer success and sales. First, concentrate on the software development part of your job. Take a couple of months to understand what's happening and then start making decisions that will change the needle. Focus on low-hanging fruit to get quick wins so others gain trust in your ability to lead.

Similar to how you started as a manager, take some time to see what's going on in R&D. Notice problems, focus on issues that matter, see if the structure the organization uses serves it, and notice whether or not the company is ready for the next level of scale.

Understand your surroundings but focus on having an amazing organization under you. The women highlighted at the beginning of this chapter weren't first timers, but rather experienced VPs. They got there by first learning the ins and outs of R&D and brought that knowledge into their roles.

Another important aspect of becoming VP is learning to work effectively with various important and high-level stakeholders.

CHAPTER 24

Working with Important Stakeholders

A colleague of mine worked for a CEO who came into work with a new idea every day. One day, he'd have a certain idea for the product, and the next he'd propose moving in a completely different direction. Not only that, but some of his decisions changed the trajectory of the product years into the future. He was driving Dina crazy.

At first, Dina argued with him because he kept changing the plan. Eventually, though, she realized that he was just talking through his ideas out loud. To avoid doing unnecessary work, Dina made a rule for herself: until the CEO talked about an idea three times, she wouldn't bother with planning or thinking about how to make it happen. She just listened.

Dina's strategy won't work for every founder, but the principle does: once you understand your founder—how he thinks, what he needs, his personality—you can figure out how to establish a smooth and efficient working relationship.

As the VP of R&D, your relationship with the founders is one of the most important. The other crucial stakeholder you'll interact with regularly is the Product department. In this chapter, we'll discuss how to work effectively with both.

WORKING WITH FOUNDERS

As discussed in the last chapter, your direct supervisor will vary depending on the size and structure of the company. In a startup or a mid-level company, you are more likely to work closely with the founders, and this relationship can pose some unique challenges.

While founders are individuals with their own personalities, they often have several attributes in common simply because they're the type of person to take a risk and start a company. For example, founders often:

- Go against the norm.
- Are smart and quick thinkers.
- Understand their own industry well.
- Lead by thinking ahead and innovating.
- Don't take things for granted; they check their assumptions about the market, their clients, how R&D works, and everything they manage.
- Don't have much experience with R&D.
- Don't have much experience managing people.

In your relationship with founders, you will probably find that you know more about some areas, especially R&D. After all, they brought you on because you are capable of running this department. At the same time, there will be areas they understand better, like running a startup. They might be younger than you or less experienced in management, but they still deserve respect for the skills they do have. You won't help your relationship by looking down on them.

WHAT DO FOUNDERS NEED FROM YOU?

Founders need to be heard, more so than a VP with tons of management experience. Founders tend to be younger and innovative, and they need to know that you understand them, their direction, and their vision for the company. You should focus on understanding their needs for the company and translate it into how you can provide that. Those needs will be specific to each company, whether it's developing features, the speed of development, or how reliable the system is.

They also need to be able to trust you. Because they don't know much about R&D, they put their confidence in you and your knowledge of your team's capacity to handle the scale needed for that product. They need you to be their partner, working with them at their fast pace.

You need to be clear with founders, giving regular reports. You should keep them up to speed with what's happening in R&D, what issues are occurring, and what you envision for the future. If you foresee needing more people on a certain project, for example, communicate that in advance.

Founders also need you to understand how they work best. They trust you to be independent and work efficiently without being closely managed. And many don't want to be bothered with issues they're expecting you to handle. Do a little inventory on the founders you work with. How much detail do they want from you? How much information about the technology do they want? How often do they want a report? Do they want your report via email or one-on-one meeting? The earlier you find out the answers to these questions, the better your working relationship will be.

I once reported to a CEO who only wanted to know the bottom line of when features were in production. While I could have bothered him with all the details about who was doing what on my team, he wasn't interested. Because I only told him the information he wanted, we worked really well together. When that startup closed, he said that if he ever launched a new company, I would be the first one he would call.

On the other hand, I worked for a CEO who wanted to know all the details of my work. He intervened with my staff and asked a lot of questions. I personally prefer to work independently, so he frustrated me. On a personal level, we got along great, but we had a strained working relationship because he wanted to be so involved. It wasn't the best fit for either of us work-wise.

UNIQUE CHALLENGES

Founders can be disorganized and might struggle to clearly define what they want. In addition, they report to a board of directors, so they might operate under pressures you don't know or understand.

Beyond that, they'll often struggle to understand why projects take as long as they do. They're more focused on their ideas and goals and might not grasp the practical side of product development. If they ask why a feature will take as long as you say it will, be prepared to explain in non-technical terms. This is especially true as the product and the company grow, because projects will probably take even more time. As the technological voice of the company, you have to explain where the project currently stands and what still needs to be done.

Starting a company isn't easy, and founders generally appreciate the people who started out early in the company with them—even if those people are unfit for their current positions. Unfortunately, if the founder wants those individuals to stay, they probably aren't going anywhere. If this happens, it's best to make peace with the situation. Perhaps you can move these people to different roles where they do less damage.

When a company has two founders, you may find yourself getting stuck in the middle of their disagreements. Your ability to do your job may be affected if they can't come to an agreement about their goals for the company and for R&D. If you start getting conflicting messages from them, set up a meeting with all three of you present. Point out that you don't want to be in the middle of their disagreement. Present your own recommendations and ask them to come to an agreement on the direction of your department. Sometimes, they will argue about issues you can't control, but you do need them to agree on your role and the goals for R&D.

Founders are often filled to the brim with thoughts: new features, timelines, people, and more. They're quick to propose new ideas, as Dina and many other VPs have learned. Don't jump to saying no. Instead, take a breath and try to understand what they *really* want. Founders don't get up in the morning with the sole goal of driving you crazy. By nature, they are often full of new ideas, and they often have additional pressures and expectations from the board of directors. By pausing to reflect on their true goals, you can often avoid stress and unnecessary actions.

Once you've considered what they really want, figure out how to say yes. Crunch the numbers: X amount of people will work Y amount of time in order to get to the goal in three months. When necessary, remind founders that production relies on a triangle: length of timeline, amount of people, and quantity of delivery. If you want to deliver more, you either need more time or more people. Similarly, if you take people out, you can't expect the same timeline and delivery amount as before. Help founders understand that while you want to meet their goal, you do have certain constraints. Work with them to figure out what is most important and come to an agreement that reflects these priorities.

WORKING WITH PRODUCT

We've talked about working with Product in previous chapters. Here, we will focus on your role as VP in this interface.

Aside from your relationship with the founders, your work with Product is most important because they define the roadmap and the features that R&D will implement. Really, the work of these two departments goes hand in hand. Make it a priority to facilitate a collaborative environment by providing frequent updates and putting Product people together with the Development teams or squads. Both groups should know why the other is doing what they're doing, how things are done, what the priorities are, and why processes take a certain amount of time. Even if they don't understand all the details, such as how technical debt works, Product should know why R&D is doing what it does. At the same time, to understand what features will help customers most, R&D needs to understand the conversation that Product has with customers.

Even though product and development go hand in hand, the relationship can be full of conflict. For example, Product often doesn't want to know the technical details, but they'll still complain that R&D has too much technical debt—even though they don't really understand why some technical features are needed. Technical debt is something only R&D will fully understand—what it means, how it's run, and how to prioritize it. Product might object because working on technical debt takes developers away from the pool, but R&D has a responsibility to insist technical debt is addressed (more on technical debt in Chapter 27). Other times, Product might complain that R&D is taking too much time to work out the bugs. When this happens, make it clear to Product that they need to prioritize fixing bugs—which might mean less content in the next sprint. Product and R&D must work together to understand each other's needs.

One of the keys to working well with Product is eliminating an "us vs. them" mentality on both sides. Foster a sense of teamwork and encourage everyone to avoid playing the blame game. If the Product team says, "Development didn't make their timelines," it's a lose-lose: the team as a whole didn't work well together and they didn't finish on time.

I have personally never had issues with the Product team. Some of this comes down to luck. If you're unlucky, you still need to work toward a positive relationship. If you're not getting along well with the Product team, consider bringing in outside counseling, people who specialize in workplace conflict. This relationship is essential to a company's success. In a healthy working relationship, every sprint starts with Product sharing what the team did, how the customers use the product, what their feedback was, what the team will do, and why they're going to do that. In response, R&D does the work to create the product and provides feedback as needed. And the final result is a happy customer and successful business. Win-win.

WORKING IN HARMONY

Being in a senior position like VP of R&D requires maturity, especially in your interfaces with important stakeholders like founders and the people in Product. The success of your department and the company as a whole, depends on your ability to establish and maintain harmonious working relationships. To do this, you need to consider the needs and motivations of other people as well as the priorities of the company. This level of maturity won't happen early on in your career, but it is something to work toward no matter where you are now.

CHAPTER 25

Working in a Startup

When you work for a large company, decisions and processes usually move at a slow, steady pace. Even if a major shift occurs, it can take years to implement.

Startups, on the other hand, move quickly. By definition, they start up and then grow and change, often rapidly and repeatedly.

Being VP of R&D in this fast-paced, ever-changing environment takes a certain set of skills, beyond those discussed earlier. You need to be flexible, calm, and cool under pressure, capable of adjusting quickly no matter what change comes your way. You also need to be skilled at growing a team that can keep up with the changes and know how to implement new features and new technology in a way that doesn't disrupt customer experience. In this chapter, you'll learn what it takes to work in a startup environment so you'll be ready if an opportunity comes your way.

HANDLING CONSTANT CHANGE

What does constant change look like in a startup? CEOs are always operating around the next round of funding, which means they think in terms of funding cycles and planning for the next stage. It also means schedules are frequently derailed by a big deal or a new investor—or the loss of one. If funding dries up, the company might pivot to another product to use technology that had been developed but not used for its original purpose. The company has to consider how to attain more customers, grow, and create more features and value—knowing that all of those plans might change based on how much funding does or doesn't bring in.

Within all of this uncertainty, as the VP of R&D, you still have to "guesstimate" how many people you will need, how much time a project will take, and so on. You might feel scared to share those estimates with the CEO, but she will appreciate the information, and she knows how things change.

In a startup, you will never have enough people, and your priorities will constantly shift, but your developers still need some level of certainty regarding the coming features and the areas of the product they will handle. It's up to you to take into account what you know right now and give them your best guess.

Sometimes, despite your best planning, you'll be asked to pivot a project while a developer is already working on it. The CEO may inform you that the feature is no longer relevant or that it's no longer a priority. If the developer has nearly finished her work, consider letting her finish. You never know when the feature might become important again. It's better to have the developer finish the work now when she has the time, because she might be working on something else when the feature becomes important again or she might have moved on to a different position. Picking the project back up, especially with a different developer, is much harder than completing it the first time around.

In addition, it's disappointing to stop a project after you've put in a lot of time, so it's better to make sure it doesn't happen over and over again, especially not to the same people.

GROWING THE TEAM

As the startup grows, your team will grow as well. This is good news, but managing a large team comes with complications.

For example, if the startup suddenly gets more funding, you might have to quickly grow your team from seven developers to twenty, as happened to me. You'll have to figure out who will mentor and teach the new people, communicate the culture of the organization and development, and ensure the newcomers follow the structure and processes of the company, such as doing code reviews for every commit to production.

Training a team of twenty developers who are up to speed and work well without needing extra hand-holding is challenging. From my experience, here's the best advice I can offer in terms of quickly growing your team.

Identify the key people and bring them into the process. Explain to them the change that is coming, listen to their concerns, and address them if possible. From the beginning, meet with these people one-on-one and as a group. Give them an opportunity to vent and take their venting seriously. Sometimes just listening is enough for them to feel better, and sometimes actions need to be taken.

Create team spirit. Keeping the lines of communication open with these key people, individually and as a group, will give them a sense of team spirit and encourage them all to keep their eyes on the goal during this growing period. It will contribute to the overall work process and morale, as well as your visibility into what's happening and how people are doing.

Watch for burnout. Know that these key people will be overworked and they might experience a lot of burnout. If that happens and no action is taken on your part, good people might leave the company. Minimize the burnout by giving them the right opportunities. This might mean having them teach new members as a group rather than individually. They can also record their lessons for newcomers to watch. Once in a while, take them off teaching duty and give them a project that really interests them.

Talk about success stories. In your one-on-ones and group meetings with these key people, celebrate successes. Talk about happy customers and improved results, and attribute these successes to specific people and thank them for their work. This will also build team spirit, reduce burnout, and energize them to keep helping you achieve the overall goal.

THE TECHNOLOGICAL ASPECTS OF YOUR ROLE

I once watched a VP change the whole product from one technology to another. He had good reasons to switch: the old technology was slow and clunky. The new technology performed well and worked well visually for customers. Additionally, it allowed the team to develop new features faster.

However, he started all new features in the new technologies without paying attention to the old features. Our team got stuck because old features were missing. Instead of transferring the old features to the new technology first and then building toward our roadmap, he launched us straight into new features with new technology. We started significantly failing on timelines. We ended up being delayed by almost a year. Even though he was a great manager, he did not handle this technology shift wisely, and he ended up being moved out of his role.

If you have to make a switch like this, consider switching the old features over to the new technology first. That way, the customers have access to the old features, only better. After the old features are working successfully with the new tech, add the new features.

Another option is to find a way for the old and new technology to work side by side rather than switching over to the new technology all at once. I've found this is the best option if possible. You'll never be able to replace everything 100 percent on a realistic timeline, so instead aim for a seamless experience for the customer. Remember that the customers don't care about if R&D switches technology; they want to use your product for its intended purpose. If you do switch technology, aim to make the customer happy and deliver the features they need. Don't interrupt the customer experience.

ARE STARTUPS FOR YOU?

I love working in startups. I love fixing big messes, building something from scratch, and solving problems quickly. Startups are less political and bureaucratic, and for me, far more exciting.

But working in a startup environment isn't for everyone. Here's another place where you have to know yourself and your skills. You might prefer being VP in a well-established company that has more stability and predictability. And that's just fine.

No matter which path you choose, being VP of R&D will have some technical aspects. In the next chapter we'll discuss how to navigate them.

IN HER WORDS: LIMOR LAHAINI

I grew up in a small town in a warm and loving family. My parents were (and still are) blue-collar workers without higher education who encouraged my siblings and me to learn and excel. They bought us our first computer when I was seven or eight years old. It was love at first sight. I was curious about how it worked and how it could be programmed, but I had no one to learn from, so I spent most of my time either playing computer games or copying programs that mostly failed.

Thirty years later, I asked my parents why they bought us a computer, when clearly it was way too expensive for them. They said they wanted us to stay at home instead of wandering around in the streets. Funny how things change: nowadays parents want their children to spend more time outside.

In sixth grade, I took my first programming course in Basic, and three years later, I joined the high school computer class and later graduated as an excellent student. After completing my MSc. in Computer Science, I got a job as a software engineer at a startup. When I told my professor, he tried to convince me to enter the PhD program instead. I eventually agreed, but I wanted to do it at the same time as my full-time job. It took me nearly three years to admit I couldn't do both and that my thesis wasn't progressing much.

By that time, it was clear to me that I was more passionate about building products than pursuing an academic career. Still, I decided to quit the job I enjoyed, so that I could obtain my PhD, which would then allow me to focus on a tech career.

From this experience I learned that sometimes I don't have to choose one thing or the other. Trying multiple options at the same time helped me understand where my passion was and what I wanted to focus on.

One month after earning my PhD in computer science, I got a job at Microsoft. I worked there for about seven years, reporting to the same manager, and then I realized I wanted a change. I didn't know exactly what I wanted, but I knew I didn't want to take my manager's place someday even though that was expected of me.

I held career discussions with my manager and with a personal coach Microsoft hired for me. They both helped me articulate what I loved about the role I had, and what I was missing in it. I loved being a technical leader, I loved the product, I loved managing people and focusing on their growth, and I loved my extended team. However, I missed working with cutting-edge technologies. I wanted to work closely with customers, and I wanted to grow my business and technical strategy skills. In addition, I wanted to "spread my wings and fly" outside of the safety net provided by my manager over the previous seven years. While I didn't aim for a specific role, knowing what I was missing made it super easy for me to apply for a position that involved building a new team in Israel, as part of a newly formed global group that codeveloped solutions with customers.

WHAT'S THE WORST THAT CAN HAPPEN?

After fourteen years at Microsoft, I was offered an opportunity to form a startup as the co-founder and CTO. My first reaction was "No way. Not now, maybe one day."

I had been promoted earlier that year, and I knew what role was designated for me next—a role that had even more responsibility but would really be more of the same. Even though I knew on some level it was time for a change, leaving to co-found the startup wasn't an option.

So, I started digging in to find what was stopping me from doing it. After all, I used to always say, "One day, I'll have my own startup."

To figure it out, I asked myself, "What's the worst thing that could happen if I left a job I enjoyed and started my own company?" Here's what I came up with:

- I could leave Microsoft, found the startup, and have it fail miserably. In that case, I would probably start looking for another job, likely in a big corporation.
- If I started interviewing, maybe I wouldn't find another job.
- If no one else hired me, I could interview at Microsoft again, and given how they appreciated me, I would most likely end up with another job at a company I loved working for.

Thinking through the worst-case scenario helped. But still, I was worried and afraid to make the move.

WHAT ARE YOU AFRAID OF?

Fear often manages us. Behind many choices that we make, or don't make, hides a fear.

I realized that one of my biggest fears about leaving Microsoft after fourteen years was finding out that I only knew how to be successful at Microsoft, and that I didn't have much worth outside that org. Realizing that, I knew I had to leave.

Over the years, I've also learned that I have intermittent imposter syndrome. At different points in my career I have worried that people would find out that I wasn't as good as they thought I was. It usually showed up when I was in a new role, surrounded by smart, experienced people I wanted to learn from. Now I have learned to embrace this feeling. It has become a kind of compass to me. When the imposter feelings start fading, I know I have grown to be as smart and experienced as the people I look up to. I have become too comfortable in my role and it's time for a change.

BE BOLD

I didn't really plan my career path; I'm more of a "go with the flow" type of person, who seeks challenges and learning opportunities. Fortunately, those chances often came my way, without much planning. Throughout my career at Microsoft, reorgs and changes in the charter provided me with growth opportunities that I found exciting. I got to design and build new products, gain experience with new technologies, lead co-engineering projects with Microsoft local startups and top global customers, and expand my scope of influence.

When it comes to product development, I have a diverse experience. I've done core algorithm development; inception and prototyping of new product ideas, maturing one of them into a new product team; incubating innovative experimental products; shipping production services for hundreds of millions of Windows users; shipping Cortana experiences; and building solutions with customers.

At different times, I've asked myself whether I should have invested in planning my career instead of going with the flow. I'd likely have moved up the ladder faster had I planned my career, and yet, I'm not convinced that would have been better. I like to think of my approach as being a different way of playing golf: instead of deciding on a specific hole and aiming for it, I decide on the shot I want to get better at and then select one or more holes that will require me to improve that shot.

In my current role as a first-time entrepreneur, my imposter syndrome is often present. I'm far from feeling I'm doing a good job, and I'm constantly doubting myself. But I remind myself that I always feel this way when I make a significant career move, and I have always succeeded. As long as I'm learning and growing, I'm doing good.

I'm a single mom by choice with a lovely boy named Ben who just turned three. Going on a startup adventure is hard, but being a single parent is way harder. This makes me feel braver and bolder when making decisions, since nothing else compares.

Find that thing that makes you feel strong, powerful, and brave, and always remember it when facing a challenge or a hard decision.

CHAPTER 26

Some Technical Aspects of Your Job

When software was first created, developers wrote the year with a two-digit marker—for example, "95" for 1995—because this took up less disc space than four digits. This worked well until the year 2000 approached and the need to switch to four digits became apparent. Software across the globe was still running on the two-digit system, impacting everything from a scheduling product such as a calendar to airplane navigation. Banks worried that software would interpret the year 00 as being a time in the past, which would impact interest calculations. Transportation services depend on accurate dates and times, so hundreds of thousands of bus, train, and plane schedules would have been affected.

To avoid these scenarios, all systems needed to work on this technical debt to address the two-digit year markers, changing it to four digits.

Y2K is the most famous example of technical debt. In this case, millions of dollars were spent to prevent the predicted catastrophes and nothing happened when the world entered the year 2000. Still, this was the responsible thing to do, as we will never know if there might have been terrible consequences if nothing had been done. Likewise, you need to take technical debt seriously at your own company, as it can have real-life consequences.

In this chapter, we'll discuss various technical aspects of your position as VP of R&D: handling technical debt, breaking up the monolith into microservices, and monitoring and alerting.

TECHNICAL DEBT AND YOU

At this point in your career, you probably know what technical debt is and have handled it in your past. If you haven't, please read this part carefully.

In designing systems, engineering groups often make technical compromises. Due to short timelines, lack of resources, or different priorities, they come up with a "good-enough" solution, knowing that at some point they will have to make some adjustments. The gap between the good-enough solution and the perfect solution is called *technical debt*, a term coined by Ward Cunningham. Eventually, the technical debt needs to be paid or you need to live with the compromise that comes with leaving it. Focus on whatever is most urgent.

As the VP of R&D, you're responsible for the technical debt of your company. You will always have some level of technical debt, so your goal isn't to make it zero. Rather, you have to know the debt, understand the implications, decide what's the most important debt to address at any given time, and take steps to handle the "repayment" in the smartest and most efficient way possible.

Your responsibility also includes telling others where the company stands in terms of technical debt. While the CEO, sales, and customer success don't necessarily care about the internals of R&D, they are impacted by technical debt. They won't be interested in the nitty-gritty details, but they should understand what the company's debt is and the consequences of not handling it—for example, not being able to serve more customers if you don't take the time to change technology that limits you from scaling the product.

HANDLING TECHNICAL DEBT

The first step in handling technical debt is identifying it every time it's created. Understand how each technical debt affects the organization and share that information with other VPs.

You can address your technical debt with a few different methods:

1. Have 20 percent of engineering tasks go toward managing technical debt on an ongoing basis, for example, on a team of five, assign one person to technical debt during each sprint.
2. Schedule a longer time period when the whole team works on addressing the debt, for example, two weeks every quarter.
3. Create a dedicated team, usually called infrastructure, whose sole job is handling technical debt and replacing technologies.

Deciding which approach to use will depend on the size of the debt. If you have a huge debt that makes it impossible to scale your product without further destabilizing it, you should focus your immediate efforts on solving that problem (option 3 above). If your product is on a good path, with the right structure and good function, then a smaller-scale solution might be a better choice, using option 1 or 2.

Regardless of how you handle it, you need to make it a regularly scheduled priority. Make sure to anticipate upcoming problems so that you can address them in a timely manner.

> ### TECHNICAL DEBT EXAMPLES
>
> Let's look at a couple of examples of technical debt and their potential impact on R&D and the company as a whole.
>
> Say you're developing a feature that runs tax calculations. During the development, you test it manually and decide not to put automatic tests into the feature so you can roll it out faster. These tests would have informed you when something fails, but they also take time to implement. Because you didn't implement the tests, you now have technical debt in that area of the product. And because of that technical debt, you run the risk of adding more code to the tax calculation feature in later releases and not knowing if you've created a regression in the code that was tested and working perfectly. As the VP, you must decide if you will dedicate the resources to creating an automatic test, or if someone will manually test the feature every time. If need be, you can also have someone run manual tests until you can dedicate a developer to creating an automatic test.
>
> Here's another example: say that you currently have X amount of data from customers coming into your system. You implement a feature that handles that amount of data perfectly, but it won't handle ten times X very well. Once the data gets to ten times X, the queue will need to be upgraded to a faster queue. You don't want to do it yet because the faster queue is more expensive, more complicated, and not yet necessary for your current amount of data. As the VP of R&D, it's your job to remember that once your data grows, you'll need to address the technical debt of the slower queue.

BREAKING UP THE MONOLITH

As mentioned earlier, for your team to work efficiently and independently from other teams, with no one stepping on each other's toes (or code), it's best to have a good microservices architecture that allows for autonomous teams, independent deployments, and the ability to use different tech stacks. After creating an API between different services, a microservices architecture also allows you to establish different timelines and development methods for different areas in your product.

If you don't currently have this kind of microservices setup, I recommend breaking up the monolith to create it. Even if you don't plan to implement the squad model discussed earlier, you'll still enjoy the benefits of having fully independent teams.

I have worked in organizations that managed breaking up the monolith in two different ways.

One approach is to break as little as possible from the monolith itself, and to create all of the new features and new areas of the product in new microservices. When a substantial change was needed in one area of the monolith, you can take the time to break it and separate this logic from the monolith.

The second approach is to do the full break all at once, so the monolith is completely broken and the new architecture serves the future features. In theory, this method is possible, but I have never seen it succeed. When I arrived at one company, they had been trying for two years to do a full break, without success. I ended up leading the company through the piece-by-piece option, and we delivered new features successfully using this approach.

While both approaches can get the job done, the first is safer and doesn't stop the whole company from engaging in new development activities. It also has less direct impact on the customers.

You can find a lot of data online on how to break the monolith into microservices, articles that will guide you through selecting the right areas to break first, the needed continuous delivery pipelines, how to make sure your business logic is kept, and so on. A whole book could be written on this topic alone.

If you need to go through this challenge, I urge you to read as many of these articles as possible to get guidelines, principles, and examples.

MONITORING AND ALERTING

Technical debt involves upcoming problems that you already know about. However, issues will arise that you can't predict. This is where monitoring and alerting come in handy.

Monitoring is a system of software components used for data collection and processing, and the presentation of the status of the system and its metrics. Alerting is the monitoring system's ability to detect and notify the operations or development team about important events that reflect problems in the system. For example, you can monitor the amount of data the system brings daily to the database, and then set an alert when the system has brought less than X items a day. Or you can monitor the time a user search took, and then set an alarm when the search took longer than your expectations from the system.

Whenever you monitor data such as this, you need to make sure the measurements are acceptable for customer use. Keep an eye on them as you scale, making sure you don't go backward and create more problems for the customer. This is especially important with critical actions of the product. For example, make sure response time experienced by customers doesn't increase as the software becomes more complicated. Ensure that your database isn't full, that services aren't down, and that the system runs and answers to you.

When unexpected issues arise, make sure to add monitoring or an alert around that area so that you can continue to track it. Every morning, you should look at a dashboard of your data so you stay in the loop. This close tracking can help you identify bugs and problems in the system so that your team can fix them before customers find them.

BE VIGILANT

Depending on your preferences, these technical aspects might be the most interesting part of your position—or boring as hell. If you find them boring, consider finding someone under you who enjoys the technical tasks and let them do it.

Regardless of how you feel about them, remember that the technical details are important and shouldn't be neglected. Be vigilant and don't skip either one.

One other technical aspect of your job involves managing data science.

CHAPTER 27

Managing Data Science

Several years ago, I managed a data science project that involved measuring the accuracy of tagging. Product wanted an algorithm that could tag whether a social media post was positive, negative, or neutral. To help the algorithm learn, people first manually tagged the data, and then the algorithm tagged new posts.

The team worked hard to tag the data and get fast results, and they achieved an amazing 76 percent accuracy, which is 6 percent higher than the industry standard.

But it wasn't good enough. Product wanted an accuracy level of at least 85 percent, and 76 percent simply wouldn't meet production needs or create customer satisfaction. The problem is that Product didn't define the needed accuracy level ahead of time. If they had, my team probably would have rejected the project up front and avoided wasting a lot of time. The team knew 70 percent accuracy was expected and if they worked miracles they might get to 75 percent, but achieving 85 percent was nearly impossible.

As VP of R&D, you will likely oversee Algorithms and Machine Learning engineering teams that implement components into product features, and as a result, you may run into situations like I did—situations that could be avoided if expectations are communicated ahead of time. Data science also includes teams that handle data analysis and business intelligence, but these often fall under the direction of the COO. In this chapter, we'll focus on the data science aspects that are part of R&D.

CONSIDERATIONS IN MANAGING DATA SCIENCE

Unlike development, data science projects are implemented with built-in uncertainty. When you start, you usually don't know if the project will succeed. You can teach the machine, and the machine will learn, but you can never be certain of the final accuracy. You don't know whether you will reach your goals and solve the problem, or reach a solution that isn't good enough to go live, as with my tagging example.

Your primary concern is the data: Is it similar to the data you will encounter in production? Is it tagged well enough? Do you have a big enough data set so that your algorithms can learn with high accuracy and create a great classifier?

One frustrating reality in working with data is that you might work really hard and take all the right actions, and still end up with poor data that results in a low accuracy level. In other cases you might get amazing results without putting in any special effort.

Developers who work with data science engineers around data science problems should be versed in the details of the project, what input the algorithm needs, and what output is expected. This helps avoid misunderstandings and wasted time along the way.

Another way to avoid misunderstandings and unnecessary complications is to involve the data science team in decision-making, to ensure their voice is heard early on. For example, data science engineers often work with data that development collected from different sources and put into a specialized database. In such cases, involve the data science team *before* development arranges the data to make sure it is done in the most usable way possible.

Unlike a lot of development features, data science algorithms can work amazingly when implemented locally by the data scientist, but work terribly in production. Don't immediately blame the algorithm and the data scientist who worked on it. The algorithm might work terribly because the data in production is very different from the data tagged months earlier to teach the algorithm. Or it might be that the tagging of the data was bad so the algorithm learned the wrong things. To preserve your relationships with data science, check all possible reasons for the result in production and don't immediately blame the people.

Data science is a rapidly changing world. Problems that could not be solved six months ago might now have a solution. Plus, data science projects are based on theoretical thinking. All of this means data scientists need to stay up-to-date on the latest advancements by reading articles and looking for different ways to approach the problems they are trying to solve.

In some cases, reading articles might not be enough and the data science team will need to consult experts in another field. For example, your team might be experts in NLP (natural language processing), and at some point, they might find themselves needing expertise in another field like image processing. Becoming knowledgeable enough could take significant time, so it might be best to consult an outside expert so that they direct you to the right area of problems to learn.

SUCCESS CHECKLIST

When you start a data science project, you can take certain steps to increase the probability of success. I am giving you my own checklist, but your specific topics and area may require additional actions.

Define the product goal for the newly discussed problem. As discussed earlier, make sure to define the accuracy level in advance. Sometimes this will make the project a nonstarter.

Discuss how much time and effort you are willing to put into the project. Once you understand the target accuracy level, decide if your data and tagging will enable you to reach this goal, and if not, how much extra effort will be required to get you there. Understanding the desired accuracy, the current data, and the time and effort required will help reduce uncertainty.

Understand how much data you need and how much you have when the project starts. The sooner the topic of data is addressed, the better vision you will have of the project. If you know you need three months' worth of human tagging to teach the algorithm, then it's best to start with that now and not with the work of the data scientists.

Check whether you can extract additional data from the data you already have. This is called feature extraction. For example, when you have an address in your data, you can enrich the data with the neighborhood name. Knowing the name would allow for more uses of the data, for instance, an insurance company could sell home insurance according to the neighborhood's quality and history of home invasions. Specific companies supply dedicated solutions designed to enrich data. See if you can use them so that your results have a higher accuracy level.

Define a sanity test for the model in advance. After you implement a model based on the algorithm's learning, you have to test the model's accuracy. Create tests that have obvious answers so that it is clear when the model fails. For example, let's say your model classifies text for sentiment—positive, negative, and neutral. Your sanity test might say, "I am happy." If the model identifies the text as negative or neutral, you know you have a huge problem.

Build a system that checks the validity of the data. If your input is speech, for example, the number of words you get in a minute should be in a specific range, and you should be alerted if this changes. If the data has some specific distribution, make sure this distribution is more or less kept in production as the result of your algorithm. If it's not, you might need to train your model again. For example, in the sentiment problem, you might reach the conclusion that 20 percent of the written text is negative, 15 percent is positive, and 65 percent is neutral. If the distribution changes drastically on certain days—for instance, 50 percent positive, 50 percent negative, and no neutral—then you need to verify that this is a real change in the data and not that the algorithm has started to fail.

Continuously check the accuracy level of the model in production. Over time, the accuracy often decreases. When this happens, retrain the model either automatically or manually.

If you follow these steps and track the various aspects of the project, you will increase the chances of its success. The other factor you have to keep in mind is timelines.

MANAGING TIMELINES

Some VPs tend to manage data science the same way they manage R&D, implementing methods like two-week sprints and rigid timelines, but this seldom works. Data science projects raise their own unique challenges because they're developing something completely different than an R&D feature, making it nearly impossible to stick to traditional timelines.

This puts you in a tricky situation: your data science team can't commit to dates, but as the senior manager in this situation, you need to commit to something. Features need to be delivered to customers by a certain date, so you need to commit timelines to the rest of the management. Also, you usually need to integrate data science with normal R&D, which does work on timelines. As the VP of R&D, you're stuck in the middle.

You can find compromise by giving structure to each data science project. For example, you might allot three to four weeks for initial research, and another three to four weeks for trying out algorithms and troubleshooting. After the given time, you can test the project for accuracy and decide if it's worthwhile to go forward with or to abandon it for a different solution.

Faced with this situation, I created a process to help meet the needs of the research team while also answering management's needs. Make sure to put timelines for each step.

- **Step 1:** Product defines the problem and describes the need.
- **Step 2:** The data science team reads relevant literature and searches for similar problems and relevant data. If they can find relevant data, it will help expedite solving the problem.
- **Step 3:** Someone, usually the development team, needs to collect the data from different sources, and then people need to tag the data—usually people outsourced for that specific task, not developers.
- **Step 4:** The data science team implements algorithms, then cleans the data. From there, they'll come back with an initial result that will help identify the accuracy level of their algorithm. At the end of this step, you'll have to decide if the accuracy level is good enough or needs improvement. If it needs improvement, brainstorm specific, different approaches. This might mean changing the definition of the problem, improving the labeling, doing more labeling, or fixing the feature that reads the data into the algorithm.
- **Step 5:** Once you achieve a good enough result, develop an API. The product can then use this new implementation. This stage is called productization because it means putting a newly implemented model into production where customers can use it.

Even with this process, it can still be difficult for your data science team to commit to timelines and accuracy. Generally, I recommend giving a time frame while knowing you need to be more flexible than with R&D. Steps 1, 2, and 4 are great markers for a timeline. At Step 4, you can put your foot down and determine if the project goes forward or not.

Usually the head of data science will have more experience in the specifics of this department. As the VP of R&D, you need to manage her and make sure she's on track with deadlines.

A BALANCING ACT

I won't lie; working in the middle between management and data science is hard. The best way to handle this balancing act is clear communication with both sides.

Represent the data science team as best you can to management. Remember that they are not in the details of the product, so they might not understand you when it comes to timelines and accuracy levels. If you set timelines with data science, keep in mind that they have to be flexible. Communicate to management what the data scientists are working on, why it's complicated, why it takes time, and why they can't commit to specific results. Remind them that sometimes it takes time to get and improve results.

On the other hand, explain to data scientists what the company's goals are and why something is or isn't acceptable. They might get a 76 percent accuracy level for a feature and think it's amazing because it's the best in the field. However, that might not cut it from the customer's perspective. Data scientists think theoretically, and your job involves making sure they are connected with reality.

CHAPTER 28

Being a Member of Company Management

In her first position as VP of R&D, Olivia stayed completely silent during management meetings. She tolerated rude and aggressive behavior like yelling and pounding on tables, and she didn't share what her department was working on or what problems R&D was facing.

As a result, when R&D missed deadlines, other departments saw this as failure on Olivia's part, even though she had good reasons for what happened. Since she didn't share, people within the company had a bad attitude toward R&D, and R&D didn't receive enough resources.

Then Olivia took a VP position at a different company. She felt more experienced when she entered this role, and successfully making the move gave her a boost of confidence. As a result,

Olivia started speaking up during meetings. It started with small steps, like simply opening her mouth to share an update. When she realized her comments were well received and got positive feedback from others, she started sharing even more. Her positive impact grew, and she slowly changed the atmosphere of the company, from frantic and scattered to calm and organized. She became the most important management member and the right hand of the CEO.

In this chapter, we'll discuss what it's like to be a member of management, both as the VP of R&D and as a woman.

MANAGEMENT MEETINGS

Though there are aspects of being a VP that are similar to being a team lead or manager, some parts of managing at this level are completely different.

One new responsibility is your weekly management meetings with all of the C-level executives and VPs in the company. During these meetings, everyone will share their department's status, challenges, and issues. You also might learn about upcoming rounds of fundraising or a new milestone number of clients.

In bigger companies, you might be one of a few VPs reporting to the SVP (senior VP). In small companies and startups, you're the only VP of R&D. Either way, you are responsible for bringing the R&D perspective to the table. Make sure that your voice is heard during management meetings. Share what's going on in R&D: timelines, measurements, the cycle of a product or feature, including how long the cycle takes, what the process is, and how you'll achieve high-quality features. If you don't take the time to educate the management team about R&D, they won't know what to expect and they won't be able to make sound decisions.

Some companies tend to focus on certain aspects of the business during these meetings: sales, marketing, and customer success. However, you need to share your department's perspective. R&D isn't the worker drone of the other departments; nothing can happen without it. As the voice of R&D, advocate for yourself and your team. Even if the bulk of the meeting is focused on the business, make sure you talk at each meeting, even if that means saying something like, "I'd like to say a few words about what's going on in R&D before we finish."

Also, pay close attention to what people share during this meeting, especially the business aspects of sales, customer success, and marketing. R&D tends to only focus on itself and Product, but the business side of the company is also important. Notice if your department can solve some of the problems they're currently having or that they see as being potential roadblocks in the near future, for example, by sharing measurements and other data. If you can help the company broadly, it will expand your perspective.

If R&D isn't given a voice during these meetings, problems will start to crop up. For example, sales might think R&D is ready to implement the necessary technology to grow from thirty clients to one hundred. If you're not, however, the production could collapse. Frame it as a discussion: sales and customer success should check in with R&D about their goals to make sure you are ready to make that happen.

BEING A MEMBER OF MANAGEMENT AS A WOMAN

At the VP level, you're often the only woman in the room. You might experience upsetting behavior from the men at this level of management, such as yelling or sexist talk. For example, a colleague of mine heard a VP say they should hire a product manager because she was "such a babe." Discussing someone's looks shouldn't be part of the hiring process, but it didn't stop this man from commenting on this applicant's appearance.

While the sexism you might experience at this level isn't necessarily worse, you don't have anyone above you to handle it. Instead, you need to stand up for yourself. Actually, you have a responsibility to call out sexism wherever you see it, even in meetings. As a member of management, it's no longer about you or your comfort level.

Be firm when you encounter unpleasant or inappropriate behavior. If someone yells during meetings, tell them not to. If someone yells at you, tell them this is the last time they are doing so and next time you will leave the room. Say it calmly and firmly. Be assertive about it. Don't stay quiet. Speak up for yourself, or female coworkers, if someone is being rude.

One colleague of mine worked at a company where everyone blamed each other. Finally, Nyra made a sign with the phrase "I'm guilty" on it. Any time the managers started blaming each other, she would pull out the sign. It changed the atmosphere by cutting the tension. Everyone laughed, but it also showed them how they were behaving.

Another colleague worked at a company that had a very high-pressure atmosphere. The more noise you could make and the more pressure you were under, the more successful you appeared within the culture of the company. Naomi, on the other hand, was very calm and organized. Her colleagues would jokingly criticize her, telling her she wasn't under enough pressure or cool enough. Rather than yelling and acting excited, she stayed calm. When the company needed a new VP of R&D, they promoted Naomi to the role. Her attitude stuck.

Sometimes, the CEO of a company with a sexist or toxic leadership team knowingly or unknowingly counts on you as a woman to change the tone. Use this to your advantage. Take the opportunity to set the tone for the team and the company, as well as your status in management.

WHERE DO YOU GO FROM HERE?

Once you've made it to VP of R&D and become a member of company management, there are few options for climbing higher within your organization. Your group could grow, which in turn becomes an advancement for you. You could also become a Chief Product Officer (CPO) and manage the VP of product and VP of R&D. Becoming an Executive VP is also an option, if your company has this position.

Not everyone wants that kind of advancement though. You might decide that your best option is to go to another company as VP of R&D, which has its own set of difficulties. No matter how you handle it, even if you do it perfectly, your decision to leave will likely be seen as a betrayal. These positions are so based on relationships and trust, that you might not be able to avoid it. I once gave a company two months' notice and they asked me to leave after ten days saying that it's bad for the group's morale that I stay.

Here's another time to "woman up" and use that self-confidence you've been working on. The pressure to stay might be great, but you have to believe in yourself and make the decision that is best for you and your career.

Conclusion

As you have seen in the stories I've included, and as you have probably experienced in your own career, being a woman in high tech and engineering comes with a unique set of challenges. It can be quite lonely at times, and that loneliness often gets worse as you advance and have fewer female peers.

One of the best ways to deal with this loneliness is to find a community of women who understand what you're going through. If possible, connect with other women inside your company. You can meet for coffee or have more formal discussions about the problems you're facing with being a working mom, discrimination, missed promotions, and more. Build each other up, encourage each other, and stand up for each other in meetings and everyday conversations whenever you have a chance.

You can also join external tech communities such as Baot and connect with a much larger group of women. These communities also have opportunities for training so that you can keep moving forward in your career. Together you can work on your struggles with self-confidence or imposter syndrome. These tech communities can help in every stage of your career.

As we grow in our careers and help other women succeed, my great hope is that we will be less alone at the top. This is one of my life's missions: to have more women at the top supporting each other.

SELF-INTROSPECTION

In addition to joining communities, take time to figure out who you are as a person and manager. Look back over the questions in Chapter 20 and write down your answers. These may change over time as you enter different roles, but at least this is a start.

Even if you are just entering your first junior software engineer position, it's valuable to think about how you work, what you expect, how you handle conflict, and so on. As discussed earlier, you want to be able to tell the story of you and your experience with confidence.

When I was advancing my career, I didn't have examples of female leaders to model my management style after. So, I created my own. I decided that I wanted to be honest and direct, saying hard things to employees and other managers when I believe they need to be said. I always give my perspective, even if the feedback is unpleasant—though I do my best to give the unpleasant feedback in the most pleasant way possible.

This doesn't have to be your style, but you should aim for businesslike and practical. It's okay to have feelings and you can be honest about them, but still remain calm and matter-of-fact when making decisions and in dealing with stressful situations.

DON'T STOP NOW

As you climb the ladder in tech, you'll see there are many other opportunities beyond the positions described here. The stories from Dalya, Rina, Ayelet, Hila, and Limor show a variety of directions your career path could take, whether it's in a big company like Dropbox or a brand-new startup or something in between.

In addition, there are opportunities for mentoring and consulting outside of your official job. Prior to writing this book, I was working as a VP of R&D on demand, serving as a temporary leader while companies who recently lost their VP searched for someone to take the position. I usually stayed for around three months and I learned a lot while I was there—all about the organization's architecture, its main problems, and the lessons they've learned.

Now I am the co-CEO of a startup, and on the side, I'm also:

- Giving lectures to women in tech, especially women in R&D about my career, my mistakes, and things I learned from them.
- Mentoring women in tech who need help in different areas.
- Consulting with CEOs and CTOs regarding R&D problems they are facing.
- Consulting with an angel investor about his seed investments, which has given me an eye-opening look at how startups pitch their ideas and how investors decide which ones are worth investing in.

I hope this book has opened your eyes to the possibilities available to you in tech and engineering. Yes, you will face challenges, but you can be brave. You can do it.

Acknowledgments

Many people helped in the creation of this book, and I would like to especially thank the following:

- Miri Curiel, Nili Davidor, Inbal Rosenshotck, and Adi Shacham Shavit, the four smart, capable VPs who contributed their knowledge and stories to the VP of R&D section.
- Rina Artstain, Ayelet Benjamini, Dayla Gartzman, Hila Noga, and Limor Lahaini, the five women who shared in their own words how they climbed the high-tech ladder.
- Dalya Garzman, Ron Gross, and Hila Noga, who reviewed the book and provided thoughtful comments.
- Haim Rapoport, my beloved brother, who read the manuscript and shared important insights.
- Rachel Ludmer, my dear friend for so many years, who provided insightful feedback on the data science chapter.
- Ron Gross, who supported me in initiating the process of writing this book.
- Eliav Alaluf, who came up with the book title.

- Gal Shalev, my ex-partner and the father of my children, for supporting me and my career every step of the way.
- Gail Fay, my amazing scribe and editor.

I would also like to thank the brave women in tech who came to me for mentoring and advice. This book would not have happened without you.

Finally, I would like to thank my family. You driving me crazy is the wind beneath my wings.

About the Author

ANAT RAPOPORT has worked her way through every rank in the engineering and technology industries. She has been VP of engineering at multiple companies and was GM and co-CEO in her last two roles. Anat is an experienced R&D manager with a master of science in computer science from Tel Aviv University. She is an Israel Defense Forces 8200 alumnus and a fierce advocate for women in tech.

Anat is a mom of three and lives in Tel Aviv, Israel, with her family.

www.ingramcontent.com/pod-product-compliance
Lightning Source LLC
Chambersburg PA
CBHW030512080526
44586CB00011B/155